THE PRUNE GOURMET

DONNA RODNITZKY / JOGAIL WENZEL / ELLIE DENSEN

CHRONICLE BOOKS • SAN FRANCISCO

Printed in the United States of America.

Library of Congress Cataloging-in-Publication Data

Rodnitzky, Donna.
  The prune gourmet / Donna Rodnitzky,
Ellie Densen, JoGail Wenzel.
    p.   cm.
  ISBN 0-87701-708-5
  1. Cookery (Prunes) I. Densen, Ellie. II. Wenzel,
JoGail. III. Title.
  TX813.P78R63 1989
  641.6'422—dc20   89-39591
                                              CIP

Cover and text design created and produced on
computer by Dare Porter / Real Time Design,
Oakland, California
Edited by Pat Tompkins

Distributed in Canada by:
Raincoast Books
112 East Third Avenue
Vancouver, B.C. V5T 1C8

10 9 8 7 6 5 4 3 2 1

Chronicle Books
275 Fifth Street, San Francisco, California 94103

This book is dedicated
to our families for their
enthusiastic support
and encouragement,
and for tasting every
recipe.

CONTENTS

CONTINUED

INTRODUCTION

What is a prune? To be exact, a prune is a dried plum. Although all prunes are plums, not all plums become prunes. Plums that become prunes are of a special species with a very high sugar content, which allows them to be dried without fermenting around the pit. Prunes grow on deciduous trees that are dormant during the winter. In the spring, blossoms appear on the trees, lasting about one week. As the blossoms fall, the new fruit is beginning to take shape and the leaf buds open.

Prunes are one of the few fruits that must fully tree ripen before they are harvested. Ripeness is determined by firmness of flesh, royal purplish color, and high natural sugar content. The orchards are ready for harvesting usually by the end of August. Modern technology has greatly facilitated prune picking. Catching frames made of fabric are placed under the trees. Mechanical shakers are then attached to the trunk or a main limb of the tree and shake the fruit off the tree. The prune plums are then taken to dehydrator yards where they are washed and dehydrated. During this process, three pounds of fresh plums become one pound of prunes.

Although the origin of the prune is not well documented, botanists have been able to trace evidence of the prune's existence in western Asia near the Caucasus Mountains bordering the Caspian Sea. The Huns, Turks, Mongols, and Tartars used prunes as a staple in their diets, most likely because this fruit was easy to transport in its dried state. The prune was then carried westward and eventually found its way to south-central and western Europe and the Balkans. However, not until 1856 were prune trees introduced to North America. Louis Pellier, a French nurseryman, came to California in 1848 in search of gold. Not being successful in this venture, he purchased land in the Santa Clara Valley in 1850 and went back into the nursery business. His brother, Pierre, joined him in 1851. A few years later Pierre returned to France to obtain a variety of fruit cuttings. The original d'Agen prune graft stock was among the selections he brought back to California. By 1900, prune orchards covered approximately 90,000 acres. Today, with improved technology, some 70,000 high-production acres produce 99 percent of all the prunes in the United States. This d'Agen prune is now known as the California French Prune.

The prune is a good source of vitamin A, iron, and potassium. It is naturally low in calories and sodium and is well recognized for being very high in both soluble and insoluble fiber. Recent medical studies have suggested that diets rich in fiber reduce the chance of intestinal diseases, such as cancer of the colon and rectum, diverticulosis, and appendicitis.

We wrote *The Prune Gourmet* for the millions of people who eat prunes daily and for those who want to begin incorporating them in their diets. Whether you choose to eat prunes simply or change them into gourmet cuisine, the recipes here will introduce you to the prune's delicious versatility.

PRUNE PREPARATION

1. **To stew prunes:** Combine prunes with equal parts water or fruit juice in a saucepan. Bring to a boil, cover, and simmer for 5 minutes. If prunes have pits, simmer for 10 minutes.

2. **To plump prunes:** Place prunes in a nonmetallic bowl and combine with an equal amount of water or juice. Cover bowl and refrigerate or let them sit on the counter overnight.

3. **To make prune juice:** Put prunes in a heavy saucepan with enough cold water to cover. Cover and refrigerate or let sit on counter overnight. The next day, bring to a boil and simmer 20 minutes. Strain.

4. **To cut prunes:** Use kitchen scissors or a knife; oil the utensil first to prevent the prunes from sticking to it.

5. **To chop prunes:** Use an electric blender or a food processor fitted with a metal blade. Use on-off pulses to coarsely chop pitted prunes. If prunes are to be used in baked goods, add a little of the flour called for in the recipe. If using pitted prunes for other kinds of recipes, add 1 tablespoon oil per pound of prunes to prevent sticking.

6. **To puree prunes:** Use an electric blender or food processor fitted with metal blade. Place drained stewed prunes in container and process until pureed. Remaining liquid may be added if recipe recommends it.

7. **To microwave prunes:** Put prunes, with enough water to cover, in a microwave-safe dish. Cover loosely with plastic wrap; cook on high for 5 minutes.

MAIN COURSES

BEEF

Brisket and Prune Tzimmes

A tzimmes is a combination of fruits or vegetables, with or without meat, cooked slowly to allow the flavors to blend. It is traditionally served on Rosh Hashanah, the Jewish New Year, because it is symbolic of the hope for a year of sweetness.
4 to 6 servings

2&2/3 cups pitted
  prunes
2 pounds boneless
  beef brisket
1 onion, sliced
2 tablespoons butter
4 large potatoes,
  peeled and quar-
  tered
1/2 teaspoon *each* salt
  and cinnamon
1/2 cup honey

Thickener:
2 tablespoons flour
2 tablespoons
  (1/4 stick) butter
1 cup pan juices
  (reserved from
  brisket and prune
  tzimmes)

Place prunes in large nonmetallic bowl and cover with water. Allow to soak several hours. Brown meat and onions in butter in Dutch oven. Add potatoes, prunes, and the water in which the prunes were soaked. Cook uncovered over moderate heat for 1 hour. Add salt, cinnamon, and honey. Stir and cover partially so that some steam may escape. Simmer an additional hour. Add water from time to time to ensure that the tzimmes remains moist and at least 1 cup of pan juices is available to add to thickener. Remove brisket and carve into thick slices. Place on warmed platter and surround with potatoes.

To make thickener: In small skillet, heat flour until it turns pale brown, stirring constantly to prevent burning. Stir in butter and slowly add pan juices, stirring constantly. When thickener is smooth, add to the prune tzimmes and stir to evenly distribute. Simmer gently 10 minutes. Serve with brisket and potatoes.

BRISKET WITH FRUIT MEDLEY

You can easily prepare this colorful and flavorful dish a day before serving it.
4 to 6 servings

1 cup *each* pitted
prunes and dried
apricots

1/2 cup *each* dried
peaches and pears

1/4 cup raisins

1 can (12 ounces)
beer (more may be
needed)

3 tablespoons dark-
brown sugar

2 tablespoons orange
marmalade

1 tablespoon brandy

1 tablespoon grated
lemon peel

Juice of 1 lemon

3/4 teaspoon ground
ginger

1/2 teaspoon cinna-
mon

1/4 teaspoon allspice

1/2 teaspoon Worces-
tershire sauce

1/2 teaspoon freshly
ground pepper

2 onions, sliced

1 3-pound boneless
beef brisket

Preheat oven to 350°.

In large saucepan, combine all ingredients, except onions and brisket. Bring to a boil over medium-high heat. Remove pan from heat and set aside.

Cut a piece of aluminum foil large enough to completely enclose and seal brisket. On foil, sprinkle half of onions in a layer about the size of brisket. Set brisket on top of onions, then sprinkle with remaining onions. Seal tightly. Set in large roasting pan and roast for 3 hours. After 3 hours, remove pan from oven. Discard foil wrapped around brisket. Spread reserved fruit mixture over brisket and cover pan with aluminum foil. Reduce oven temperature to 300° and roast another hour, adding more beer if sauce becomes dry.

To serve, place brisket on heated platter and surround with fruit and sauce.

GERMANTOWN BEEF STEW
4 to 6 servings

1&1/2 cups sliced
onions

2 tablespoons
vegetable oil

1&1/2 pounds lean
beef chuck, cut in
1&1/2-inch cubes

2&3/4 cups water

1 cup apple juice

1 teaspoon salt

1/4 teaspoon freshly
ground pepper

1 bay leaf

2 large carrots, sliced
diagonally 1/4 inch
thick

1&1/2 cups pitted
prunes, halved

1/4 cup cider vinegar

1&1/2 tablespoons
flour

1/2 teaspoon ground
ginger

3 tablespoons chopped
parsley

In Dutch oven, sauté onions in oil over medium heat 5 minutes. Increase heat to high; add beef and stir until browned, about 10 minutes. Add water, juice, salt, pepper, and bay leaf. Bring to boil; reduce heat and simmer about 1&1/2 hours, stirring occasionally, until beef is nearly tender. Add carrots; simmer 15 minutes. Add prunes; simmer 10 minutes more.

In small bowl, combine vinegar, flour, and ginger; mix until smooth. Gradually stir into beef mixture; simmer 10 minutes. Remove and discard bay leaf. Stir in parsley just before serving.

GRILLED TERIYAKI STEAK

*Add a little flavor of the Far East to your next
cookout. Serve with stir-fried vegetables, rice,
and a bowl of hot deep-fried wonton wrappers
lightly sprinkled with salt.*
4 to 6 servings

Marinade:
3/4 cup salad oil
1/2 cup soy sauce
1 cup prune juice
2 tablespoons honey
2 tablespoons vinegar
1&1/2 teaspoons
   ground ginger
1 garlic clove, mashed
1 green onion,
   chopped

1 3-pound flank steak

Combine marinade ingredients in large bowl.
Whisk until well blended. Place steak in non-
metallic baking dish and cover with marinade.
Refrigerate, covered, 8 hours or overnight.

Remove from refrigerator 1 hour before serving.
Grill 5 to 6 minutes on each side. Brush frequently with marinade. Steak should be medium rare and sliced diagonally in thin slices.

Hungarian Beef Stew with Dried Fruits

1/2 pound bacon, cut into 1/2-inch pieces

1 cup flour

3 pounds beef chuck, cut into 2-inch pieces

6 tablespoons oil

1/2 teaspoon cinnamon

Salt and freshly ground pepper

3 medium-size onions, thinly sliced

3 large garlic cloves, minced

6 tablespoons tomato paste

1&1/2 teaspoons Hungarian sweet paprika

1&1/2 cups dark beer

1 cup beef stock

1/2 cup prune juice

2/3 cup *each* pitted prunes and dried apricots

1/3 cup dried apples

1/3 cup currants

1/2 teaspoon thyme

1 bay leaf

2 tablespoons fresh lemon juice

This hearty stew is perfect for winter dinners. Accompany it with salad and pumpkin bread.
6 servings

In pan of boiling water, blanch bacon 5 minutes. Drain and set aside.

Put 1 cup of flour in brown paper bag. Shake half of beef pieces in bag to coat. Set floured pieces aside. Repeat process with remaining beef. Over medium-high heat, heat oil in Dutch oven. Add half of beef pieces to Dutch oven. Sprinkle with half of cinnamon, salt, and pepper and cook 10 minutes or until beef is crisply browned. Transfer to platter, using slotted spoon. Follow the same procedure with remaining beef.

To same Dutch oven, add bacon and onions. Cook 10 minutes, or until onions are translucent, stirring constantly. Add garlic and cook 2 minutes, stirring constantly. Stir in tomato paste, paprika, beer, stock, and prune juice and boil 5 minutes or until reduced by half. Add dried fruits, beef, thyme, and bay leaf. Reduce heat, cover partially, and simmer about 2&1/4 hours or until beef is almost tender. Add lemon juice and peel. Continue cooking, uncovered, until beef is tender, about 15 minutes. Remove and discard bay leaf.

CONTINUED

1 tablespoon grated
lemon peel

Sour cream (optional)

Optional: You may garnish each serving with a dollop of sour cream.

If you make this stew the day before serving it, refrigerate it; rewarm over medium-low heat, stirring often.

Pot Roast with Prunes

For a delightful Sunday supper, serve with buttered noodles or German potato pancakes. The sauce is fantastic.
6 to 8 servings

1 4-pound rump roast
3 tablespoons oil
2 medium-size
  onions, sliced
2/3 cup pitted prunes
4 whole cloves
Salt and freshly
  ground pepper
1 cup *each* water and
  cider

In large Dutch oven, brown meat on all sides in hot oil. Add onions. Cook, stirring frequently until browned. Add remaining ingredients. Reduce heat to a simmer, cover, and cook until meat is tender, 3 to 4 hours. Add more water as necessary to prevent meat from sticking. Strain sauce from the Dutch oven to remove and discard cloves. Serve warm with sauce on the side.

PRUNE ORCHARD BEEF STEW

1&1/2 pounds lean chuck beef, cut into 1-inch cubes

2 tablespoons flour

3 tablespoons vegetable oil

1 large onion, sliced

1&1/4 cups *each* prune juice and water

1 teaspoon salt

1/2 to 1 teaspoon thyme

1/4 to 1/2 teaspoon freshly ground pepper

3 medium potatoes, peeled and sliced 1/4 inch thick

3 large carrots, sliced diagonally 1/4 inch thick

3 tablespoons lemon juice

1 teaspoon grated lemon peel

3 tablespoons chopped parsley for garnish

The rich, fruity flavor of prune juice transforms ordinary beef stew into a deliciously exotic entrée.

4 to 6 servings

Dredge beef with flour. Heat oil in Dutch oven over high heat. Add beef; stir until browned. Add onion, prune juice, water, salt, thyme, and pepper. Bring to boiling; reduce heat, cover, and simmer gently until beef is just tender, 1 to 1&1/2 hours. Mix in potatoes, carrots, and lemon juice and peel. Cover and simmer until potatoes and carrots are tender, about 20 minutes. Sprinkle each serving with parsley.

Savory Beef Ragout

4 medium-size
potatoes, peeled and
cut into 1-inch
cubes

6 carrots, sliced into
1-inch pieces

2 medium-size
onions, cut into
chunks

2 pounds beef stew
meat, cut into
1-inch cubes

1 can (8 ounces)
tomato sauce

1&1/2 cups dry red
wine

2 tablespoons wine
vinegar

1 tablespoon brown
sugar

1 teaspoon salt

1 garlic clove, mashed

1/4 teaspoon freshly
ground pepper

1 1-inch stick
cinnamon

1/2 teaspoon whole
cloves

1 bay leaf

1/4 cup *each* raisins,
pitted prunes, and
dried apricots

This spicy stew is chock-full of dried fruits and vegetables. Serve with green salad and vinaigrette and coarse peasant bread.
6 servings

In large Dutch oven, thoroughly combine all ingredients. Bring to a boil, cover, and simmer over low heat for 3 to 4 hours. Before serving, remove cinnamon stick, cloves, and bay leaf.

TERIYAKI HAMBURGERS

Serve these hamburgers at your next luau or barbecue.
6 servings

Hamburgers:
3 pounds lean ground
  beef
1/2 cup soy sauce
2 tablespoons sherry
1 cup prune juice
2 tablespoons sugar
1 garlic clove, mashed
1/2 teaspoon ground
  ginger

Chutney Butter:
1/2 cup (1 stick)
  butter, room tem-
  perature
1/4 cup chutney
1/4 cup chopped
  parsley

Hamburger buns
1 can pineapple rings,
  drained
Green onions,
  diagonally sliced
1 green pepper cut
  into strips

Combine hamburger ingredients in large bowl until thoroughly blended. Cover and refrigerate overnight or several hours.

When ready to serve, combine chutney butter ingredients. Spread insides of buns with thin layer of chutney butter. Place buns butter side up under broiler and broil until lightly toasted. Set aside.

Form hamburger mixture into patties. Grill until done. Serve on buns and top with pineapple rings, green onions, and green pepper.

Note: Blue-Ribbon Chutney on page 212 is a good choice for the chutney butter.

LAMB

INDIAN LAMB CURRY

Make this dish ahead for a crowd and enjoy a carefree dinner party. Serve with rice, fruit, and bowls of chutney, coconut, sliced bananas, and peanuts.
8 servings

2 cups hot milk

1 cup fresh or dried
coconut, shredded

6 tablespoons
(3/4 stick) butter

2&1/2 pounds boned
lamb shoulder, cut
into cubes

2 onions, chopped

1 green pepper,
chopped

1 garlic clove, mashed

1/4 cup curry

2 teaspoons *garam
masala*

2 tart green apples,
chopped

1/2 cup raisins

1 cup prunes, cut into
raisin-size pieces

2 tablespoons flour

1 cup chicken broth

1/4 cup mango
chutney

Salt to taste

Red pepper flakes to
taste, optional

Combine hot milk with coconut in small bowl. Set aside.

Melt butter in Dutch oven. Add lamb and sauté until brown. Remove lamb with slotted spoon and set aside. Add vegetables and garlic to Dutch oven and sauté until onions are translucent. Add curry and garam masala and combine well. Add fruits; sprinkle with flour, and stir in chicken broth and coconut milk mixture. Stir in lamb and simmer, uncovered, 20 to 30 minutes or until lamb is tender. Add chutney, salt, and optional red pepper.

Note: Garam masala is an Indian curry containing as many as 15 spices that can be purchased at most Asian grocery stores.

MARION'S BOBOTIE

1 large onion,
chopped
1 tablespoon butter
1 large tart green
apple, cut into
1-inch cubes
1 pound ground lamb
2 slices whole-wheat
bread, soaked in
water to cover
2 tablespoons curry
powder
2 tablespoons apricot
jam
1 cup raisins
3/4 cup pitted prunes,
chopped
1/3 cup dried apricots
1/2 cup almonds,
chopped
1/3 cup apple cider
vinegar
3 bay leaves
Salt and freshly
ground pepper to
taste
1 egg

Egg Glaze:
1 egg
1/4 cup milk

Our friend Marion, who hails from Botswana, shared this recipe with us. She claims it is the African answer to American meatloaf. With the addition of prunes, it far surpasses any meatloaf we've ever had.
4 servings

Preheat oven to 350°.

Sauté onion in butter until translucent. Add apple and cook, stirring constantly for 1 minute. Add lamb to onion mixture and cook until no longer pink. Pour off any excess fat. Squeeze water out of bread, tear bread into pieces, and add to lamb, stirring for 2 minutes. Add remaining ingredients. Combine well and put into 2-quart casserole dish. Cover and bake for 50 minutes.

Whisk together egg glaze ingredients and pour over casserole. Bake uncovered for an additional 10 minutes. This dish is delicious served over white rice cooked with turmeric. Encourage dinner guests to be creative with condiment bowls filled with Peachy Chutney, sliced bananas, plain yogurt, and chopped tomatoes combined with diced onions.

Note: See page 221 for Peachy Chutney.

Moroccan Couscous and Lamb

A complete dinner in one pot. Serve leftovers stuffed in pita bread for a great lunch or midnight snack.
6 servings

2/3 cup quick-cooking couscous
1 cup mixed dried fruit, cut into small pieces
2 cups boiling chicken stock
1/4 cup olive oil
1 pound ground lamb
3 large garlic cloves, finely chopped
Salt
6 medium-size green onions, chopped
6 carrots, thinly sliced
1 tart green apple, cored and coarsely chopped
1 red bell pepper, coarsely chopped
1/4 cup almonds, slivered
2 teaspoons fresh lemon juice
1 teaspoon cinnamon
1/4 teaspoon cayenne pepper

Place couscous and dried fruit in small bowl. Pour 3/4 cup boiling stock over mixture and stir to blend. Cover bowl and set aside.

In Dutch oven, heat oil over high heat. Add lamb, garlic, salt, and onions and stir for 15 seconds. Lower heat to medium setting and add carrots. Cover Dutch oven and cook until lamb is no longer pink, about 4 minutes. Stir occasionally to prevent meat from burning. Add couscous mixture and remaining ingredients and blend well. Cover again and cook an additional 10 minutes or until mixture is just heated through, stirring occasionally. Add more stock as necessary to keep couscous moist. Serve immediately.

SIMPLE LAMB CURRY

Transform lamb into a spicy meal.
4 servings

2 tablespoons oil
2 medium onions, chopped
1 green pepper, chopped
2 tart green apples, chopped
1 garlic clove, mashed
2 tablespoons *each* flour and curry powder
1/2 teaspoon *each* salt, marjoram, and thyme
1 cup chicken broth
1/2 cup dry white wine
1/2 cup *each* raisins and pitted prunes, cut into raisin-size pieces
1/4 cup sweetened coconut, shredded
3 cups cooked lamb, cut into 1-inch cubes
1/4 cup sour cream *or* unflavored yogurt

In Dutch oven, heat oil and sauté onions, green pepper, apples, and garlic until onions are translucent. Add flour and spices to vegetables and stir. Add chicken broth, wine, and fruit and bring to a simmer. Stir in coconut and lamb and heat through. Just before serving, blend in sour cream or yogurt. Serve over rice.

MAIN COURSES

PORK

Continental Chops with Prunes

A simple but elegant dinner that will please friends as well as family. Serve with steamed new potatoes, salad, and French bread.
4 servings

2 tablespoons
(1/4 stick) butter
1 *each* carrot, onion,
and celery stalk,
chopped
4 sprigs parsley,
minced
1 bay leaf
1/4 teaspoon dried
thyme
1 garlic clove, minced
Salt and freshly
ground pepper
2 tablespoons red
wine vinegar
3/4 cup dry red wine
1&1/3 cups pitted
prunes
3 tablespoons butter
1 tablespoon vegetable
oil
4 center-cut loin pork
chops
1 tablespoon butter,
room temperature
1 tablespoon flour
Chopped parsley for
garnish

To make sauce, melt 2 tablespoons butter in medium saucepan. Add vegetables, herbs, and spices. Sauté them until soft. Add vinegar and red wine and simmer 20 minutes. Strain sauce, discarding vegetables, and return remaining liquid to saucepan. Set aside.

In medium saucepan, place prunes with enough water to cover and simmer 20 minutes. Drain and keep prunes warm.

In large frying pan, heat 3 tablespoons butter and oil. Add pork chops, seasoning them with salt and pepper, and sauté until brown on both sides. Remove to heated platter and keep warm. Blend 1 tablespoon butter and flour together to make a paste. Add in small increments to the reserved sauce and cook gently for a few minutes until it thickens, stirring constantly. Add warm prunes to sauce and taste for seasoning. Pour sauce and prunes over pork chops and sprinkle with chopped parsley.

COUNTRY BAKED SPARERIBS

These spicy ribs are glazed with a sweet-and-sour prune sauce reminiscent of lazy summer days and southern hospitality.
8 servings

6 pounds pork
  spareribs
1&1/2 cups pitted
  prunes
1&1/2 cups water
1 cup sliced onions
2 garlic cloves, sliced
1 teaspoon salt
1/4 teaspoon *each*
  freshly ground
  pepper and ground
  ginger
2&1/2 tablespoons
  cider vinegar
1 tablespoon honey

Preheat oven to 350°.

Place ribs on racks in shallow baking pans. Bake for 1 hour. Meanwhile, in 2-quart saucepan, combine prunes, water, onions, garlic, and spices. Bring to boil, reduce heat, and simmer about 15 minutes, stirring occasionally, until prunes are soft. Pour into container of electric blender; add vinegar and honey. Blend until smooth, scraping sides of container as needed. Generously spread prune mixture over ribs to coat top surface. Return ribs to oven for about 30 minutes until tender. To serve, cut between ribs.

Family Favorite Chops

4 to 6 servings

1/4 cup oil

6 loin pork chops

Salt and freshly
  ground pepper

2 onions, quartered

1 can (10&3/4
  ounces) chicken
  broth

Juice and finely grated
  peel of 1 lemon

1 cup pitted prunes

1 teaspoon ground
  cloves

4 large potatoes,
  peeled and quar-
  tered

4 large carrots, halved

1/2 cup chopped
  parsley

In large skillet, heat oil and brown chops on both sides over medium heat. Season with salt and pepper. Remove chops from pan with slotted spoon.

In same pan, cook onions until translucent. Add chicken broth and simmer over high heat, scraping sides and bottom of pan to loosen food particles. Stir in lemon juice and peel. Return chops to pan and add remaining ingredients. Bring liquid to boil, cover tightly, reduce heat, and simmer for 45 minutes or until chops and vegetables are tender.

GOURMET PORK LOIN

This is an elegant dish.
6 to 8 servings

12 pitted prunes

Dry Madeira

1 large tart green
apple, peeled

1 teaspoon lemon
juice

4&1/2 to 5 pounds
boned loin of pork,
preferably center
cut

3 tablespoons *each*
butter and oil

1/2 cup dry white wine

3/4 cup whipping
cream

1&1/4 tablespoons red
currant jelly

Place prunes in a nonmetallic bowl. Add enough Madeira to cover and set aside for 4 to 6 hours or overnight. Drain prunes, reserving Madeira, and pat dry.

Cut apple into 1-inch pieces and sprinkle with lemon juice. Using a sharp knife, make a hole in the center of each end of the pork loin. Push the handle of a wooden spoon through entire length of loin, turning to make a tunnel approximately 1/2 inch in diameter. Alternately stuff prunes and apple cubes into tunnel, pushing from both ends. Sew openings shut at both ends with poultry lacer or large needle and heavy thread.

Preheat oven to 350°.

In large Dutch oven, melt butter and oil. When foam subsides, add pork loin and brown evenly on all sides. Remove pork and set aside. Pour fat from Dutch oven and discard. Add white wine and reserved Madeira to Dutch oven, then whisk in cream. Bring to a simmer on top of stove. Return pork to Dutch oven. Cover and bake in oven for 1&1/2 hours or until meat shows no resistance when pierced with tip of sharp knife. Remove pork loin to a heated

platter, remove thread, and carve into slices.
Keep warm. Skim fat from liquid in pan. Bring
liquid to boil and reduce to 1 cup, stirring
constantly. Add jelly and stir until smooth.
Pour gravy into heated sauceboat and serve with
pork loin.

HUNGARIAN PORK STROGANOFF

You can prepare this easy recipe a day before serving it. Served over noodles, with peas and crusty bread, this is a hearty meal.
4 servings

1/4 cup flour seasoned with salt, freshly ground pepper, and Hungarian sweet paprika
2 pounds boneless pork shoulder, cut into 1-inch cubes
1/4 cup (1/2 stick) butter
2 medium-size onions, diced
2 tablespoons peeled, minced gingerroot
1 cup fresh mush-rooms, sliced
1/2 cup pitted prunes
2&1/2 cups dry white wine
1/2 cup whipping cream

Put flour, salt, pepper, and paprika in small brown paper bag. Add pork cubes and shake until well dusted. In Dutch oven, heat butter over moderately high heat and brown pork in batches, transferring to bowl with slotted spoon. Sauté onions in same pan, adding more butter if necessary. Add gingerroot and return pork to pan. Cook mixture, stirring for 1 minute. Add mushrooms, prunes, and wine and simmer mixture, covered, for 1&1/2 hours. Stir in cream just before serving.

Pork Medallions in Crème Fraîche

Serve this sophisticated but easy dish with asparagus and sautéed new potatoes.
6 to 8 servings

2 cups pitted prunes

2 cups medium dry white wine

2 pork tenderloins

3/4 teaspoon ground ginger

1/2 teaspoon salt

1/8 teaspoon white pepper

1/2 cup flour

1/4 cup (1/2 stick) butter

2 tablespoons red currant jelly

1&1/4 cups *crème fraîche*

Rosemary sprigs for garnish

Cook prunes and wine in a medium-size saucepan for 10 minutes over medium heat. Strain prunes, reserving liquid.

Cut tenderloins into slices 1/2 inch thick. Put ginger, salt, white pepper, and flour in small brown paper bag. Add tenderloin slices and shake to coat. Melt butter in heavy-bottom frying pan and sauté tenderloin pieces until browned on both sides. Add reserved liquid and simmer 5 minutes or until meat is cooked through. With slotted spoon, transfer the medallions to a warm serving dish, retaining the juices in the pan. Arrange prunes around medallions. Keep warm.

Add jelly to pan juices and bring to a boil, stirring constantly until syrupy. Slowly add crème fraîche and stir until thick. Pour over pork. Garnish with rosemary sprigs.

Note: Crème fraîche is a tart, thick cream frequently used in French recipes. You can find it in the dairy section in most large supermarkets. To make your own créme fraîche: Combine 1&1/4 cups whipping cream and 1&1/4 teaspoons buttermilk in a glass jar and cover with plastic wrap. Let sit at room temperature for 24

CONTINUED

to 36 hours or until the consistency of sour cream. Refrigerate for at least 24 hours before using.

ROAST LOIN OF PORK WITH PRUNE FILLING

Accompany this pork roast with avocado and grapefruit salad, wild rice, and sourdough bread.
6 servings

Preheat oven to 350°.

2&1/2 pounds
  boneless pork loin
3/4 cup pitted prunes
Salt and freshly
  ground pepper to
  taste
1 teaspoon oil
2 tablespoons
  (1/4 stick) butter
1/2 cup water
1/2 teaspoon thyme
1 bay leaf
1 tablespoon chopped
  parsley

Using a sharp knife, make a hole in the center of each end of the pork loin. Push the handle of a wooden spoon through entire length of loin, turning to make a tunnel approximately 1/2 inch in diameter. Stuff prunes into tunnel, pushing from both ends. Sew openings shut at both ends with poultry lacer or large needle and heavy thread. Season pork with salt and pepper.

In large casserole over medium-high heat, melt the oil and butter. Add the roast to the casserole and brown it on all sides. Add water and herbs and bring to a boil. Place casserole in oven and roast for 60 to 70 minutes, basting every 15 minutes with pan juices, adding water as necessary.

Transfer pork to cutting board and let rest 10 minutes before removing thread and cutting into slices. Arrange slices on a heated platter. Remove bay leaf from pan juices and skim off fat. Serve sauce separately in a gravy boat.

SENSATIONAL SAUSAGE PIE

This is one of our favorite recipes. Serve warm with crisp, green salad or tuck in hamper for a French picnic in the woods.
6 to 8 servings

Filling:

2/3 cup *each* pitted prunes, dried apricots, and apples, chopped

1 cup dry white wine

1 tablespoon butter

1 large onion, chopped

2 tablespoons brandy

2 tart green apples, peeled and finely chopped

1 pound cooked kielbasa sausage, coarsely chopped

1/2 cup sauerkraut, thoroughly rinsed and drained

3 cups Swiss cheese, shredded

Salt and freshly ground pepper

To make filling: Combine fruits and wine in small saucepan over low heat until hot to touch. Remove from heat and let mixture cool to room temperature.

In large skillet, melt butter over medium-high heat. Add onion and sauté until browned. Drain wine from fruit and pour into skillet. Increase heat to high; add brandy and boil, stirring constantly until reduced to thin glaze. Remove pan from heat and stir in dried fruit, apples, sausage, and sauerkraut. Let cool to room temperature. Stir in cheese. Season with salt and pepper. Set aside.

To assemble crust: In work bowl of food processor, process flour and salt. Add butter and yolk and process until mixture resembles coarse cornmeal. Add ice water and continue processing until dough forms into a ball. Additional water may be added if dough seems dry or does not readily form into ball. Wrap dough in plastic wrap and refrigerate 10 minutes. Place two thirds of dough on a floured surface and roll into 14-inch circle. Press circle into bottom of well-greased 11 x 1-inch tart pan with removable bottom. Trim edges with scissors, leaving

Crust:

3 cups flour

3/4 teaspoon salt

1 cup plus 2 table-
spoons (2&1/4
sticks) butter, well
chilled and cut into
small pieces

1 extra large egg yolk

4&1/2 tablespoons ice
water

1 egg beaten with 1
teaspoon cold water

a generous 1/2 inch of pastry. Spoon filling evenly over bottom crust. Fold 1/2 inch of pastry over outer edge of filling and brush pastry lightly with water. Roll out remaining dough into 13-inch circle and place over filling, centering it carefully. With fingers, press down on rim of tart pan to cut off excess pastry. Using back of fork tines, press around edge of pastry to seal crust. Make a few slits in top of crust. Reroll scraps of dough and cut into leaf shapes to decorate top of pie.

Preheat oven to 375°.

Brush pie with beaten egg. Bake for about 1 hour or until golden brown. Cool 20 minutes in pan. Remove outer ring from pan and serve.

Note: You can make the crust without a food processor as follows. In large bowl, combine flour and salt. Using pastry blender, cut in butter until mixture resembles coarse cornmeal. Add egg yolk and ice water. Stir with fork until dough forms into a ball.

TIPSY PORK ROAST WITH DRIED FRUIT

2 3- to 4-pound
boneless pork loins
1 teaspoon allspice
1/2 teaspoon freshly
ground pepper
2 large garlic cloves,
slivered
2 tablespoons *each*
butter (1/4 stick)
and oil
1&1/2 cups chicken
broth
3 medium-size
onions, peeled and
halved
1 cup *each* pitted
prunes and dried
apricots, quartered
1/4 cup sugar
1/4 cup red wine
vinegar
2 cups chicken broth
1 tablespoon corn-
starch dissolved in 1
tablespoon apricot
liqueur
1/2 cup apricot
liqueur
Salt and freshly
ground pepper
Fresh lemon juice

An unusual pork roast that is perfect to serve for that special dinner party. Accompany it with a green salad, rice pilaf, and French bread. **12 servings**

Rub roasts with allspice and pepper. Make a number of slits in the roasts with the point of a knife and insert garlic slivers in the slits. Set aside for 2 hours.

Preheat oven to 375°.

In large, heavy roasting pan, melt butter and oil over medium-high heat. Brown roasts on all sides in pan. Discard fat from pan and add 1&1/2 cups chicken broth and onions to roasts. Insert meat thermometer in one roast and cook for 30 minutes per pound or until thermometer registers 170°. Baste frequently. Cover pan with aluminum foil the last 30 minutes.

Prepare sauce by first combining fruit in glass bowl with enough boiling water to cover. Let stand 30 minutes. Drain and set fruit aside.

In heavy medium-size saucepan over low heat, heat sugar and vinegar until sugar dissolves. Increase heat and boil 5 minutes or until it becomes a richly colored brown syrup. Carefully stir in 2 cups chicken broth and simmer 3 minutes. Blend in dissolved cornstarch and simmer an additional 1 to 2 minutes or until sauce is clear and thickened.

Remove roasts to heated platter and cover them to keep warm. Discard onion and fat from pan. Place pan over medium heat and add liqueur and thickened broth, stirring with a wooden spoon to scrape up any browned bits. Bring to a rolling boil. Add drained fruit and heat through. Season with salt, pepper, and lemon juice.

Carve roasts into slices 1/2 inch thick and return to platter. Ladle fruit and part of sauce over roasts. Serve accompanied with remaining sauce in sauceboat.

TROPICAL KEBABS

Colorful, tasty, and easy—just right for a summer barbeque.
6 to 8 servings

Marinade:

6 tablespoons hoisin
  sauce

1 cup prune juice

1 tablespoon soy sauce

3 tablespoons apricot
  preserves

Kebabs:

3 pounds pork
  tenderloin, cut into
  1-inch cubes

4 red bell peppers, cut
  into 1-inch squares

48 pitted prunes

1 fresh pineapple, cut
  into chunks

In small bowl, whisk together ingredients for marinade. Pour over pork cubes and marinate, covered, 6 hours in refrigerator, turning pork cubes twice.

One hour before grilling, place pork, peppers, prunes, and pineapple on skewers. Brush with marinade and let sit in refrigerator 1 hour. Grill 4 to 5 minutes on each side, brushing frequently with marinade. Serve on bed of pilaf.

Note: Hoisin sauce is a spicy sauce that you can find in most larger supermarkets or Asian groceries.

POULTRY

Chicken Breasts with Curried Vegetables

Fragrant with a piquant curry sauce, this colorful main course is high in nutrition, low in fat.
4 servings

2 tablespoons
(1/4 stick) butter
4 chicken breast
halves, skinned and
boned
1 teaspoon curry
powder
1 garlic clove, pressed
1/4 cup dry vermouth
or dry white wine
1/2 teaspoon salt
1/2 cup pitted prunes
2 cups sliced vege-
tables (onions,
mushrooms, zuc-
chini, bell peppers,
or broccoli)

In large heavy skillet, melt butter over medium heat. Add chicken; sauté until light brown on both sides. While browning chicken, stir curry powder and garlic into butter. Add vermouth, salt, and prunes. Cover; simmer over low heat 5 to 7 minutes. To test doneness, press finger into thickest part of chicken breast; meat should spring back. Place chicken on a plate and cover with skillet lid to keep warm. Add vegetables to pan juices; stir. Cook until tender-crisp. Spoon vegetables and juices over chicken and serve.

CHICKEN CREOLE

All this dish needs is some accompanying rice to make it a hearty meal.
4 servings

1 cup pitted prunes, chopped
1 cup hot chicken broth
3 pounds boned, skinned chicken breasts, cut into cubes
2 tablespoons oil
1 large onion, chopped
1 large green bell pepper, cut into squares
1 large red bell pepper, cut into squares
1/4 cup finely chopped celery
2 garlic cloves, chopped
1 can (16 ounces) whole tomatoes, broken up
1/2 teaspoon salt
1 teaspoon dried basil
1/4 teaspoon freshly ground pepper
1/2 teaspoon dried thyme
Dash of Tabasco

In small nonmetallic bowl, combine prunes and chicken broth. Set aside.

In large frying pan, sauté chicken pieces in oil until white. Remove chicken from pan with a slotted spoon and set aside. In same pan, sauté onion, peppers, celery, and garlic until softened, about 5 minutes. Add remaining ingredients and simmer for 10 minutes or until thick. Return chicken to pan to heat through. Serve on a bed of rice.

CHICKEN JUBILEE

Serve this colorful dish with lemon rice, sautéed snow peas, and Buttermilk-Prune Muffins (page 97).
8 servings

2 frying chickens, cut into serving-size pieces
Salt and freshly ground pepper
Garlic powder to taste
1/2 cup (1 stick) butter, melted

Place chicken, skin side up, in large roasting pan. Sprinkle with salt and pepper. Mix garlic powder and butter; brush over chicken. Broil chicken until brown, watching carefully to prevent burning. Remove pan from oven and set aside.

Preheat oven to 325°.

Sauce:
1 cup water
2 medium-size onions, sliced
1/2 cup *each* raisins and pitted prunes, chopped
1/2 cup light-brown sugar
1 bottle (12 ounces) chili sauce
1 tablespoon Worcestershire sauce
1 cup dry sherry
1 can (17 ounces) pitted Bing cherries, drained

In medium saucepan, combine all sauce ingredients except sherry and cherries. Cook over medium heat for 5 minutes. Pour over chicken, cover pan tightly with foil, and bake for 1 hour. Remove foil, add sherry and cherries, and return to oven, uncovered, for 15 minutes.

CHICKEN WITH PRUNES AND APRICOTS

Serve this peasant dish with spicy brown rice, spinach salad, and coarse whole wheat bread.
4 servings

1 tablespoon oil
1 cup sliced onions
4 chicken breasts, skinned and boned
Paprika
1/2 cup *each* dried apricots and pitted prunes, halved
1&1/2 cups chicken stock
2 tablespoons lemon juice
1/2 teaspoon dill weed
1 teaspoon cinnamon
1&1/2 teaspoons cornstarch
1/4 cup cold water

In frying pan, heat oil and sauté onions until soft. Add chicken and sprinkle with paprika. Sauté 3 minutes on each side. Add fruit, chicken stock, lemon juice, dill weed, and cinnamon. Bring to a simmer, cook uncovered 20 minutes. Mix cornstarch and water, add to chicken mixture, and stir gently. Cook until sauce thickens; serve with pilaf.

Glazed Chicken with Sweet Potatoes

4 servings

1 cup pitted prunes

1/4 cup raisins

1 cinnamon stick

4 chicken breasts

1 tablespoon butter

Salt and freshly
    ground pepper

1 can (12 ounces)
    sweet potatoes,
    drained

In small saucepan, combine prunes, raisins, and cinnamon stick with water to cover. Bring to a boil and simmer 10 minutes. Drain prunes and raisins, reserving liquid. Remove cinnamon stick. Puree prunes and raisins in food processor or blender with 3 tablespoons of reserved liquid.

Preheat oven to 350°.

Lightly oil medium-size casserole dish. Put chicken into casserole. Rub with butter and season with salt and pepper. Spread some of the prune puree over chicken. Cover casserole and bake for 45 minutes. Remove casserole from oven and arrange sweet potatoes around chicken. Baste with puree. Bake uncovered for 15 more minutes, basting several times with puree.

NEW DELHI CHICKEN

An easy dish to prepare for your family. Serve with rice, fresh fruit, and corn muffins.
6 servings

1/3 cup oil

2 medium-size
onions, chopped

1 garlic clove, minced

1 cup boiling water

2 tablespoons fresh
lemon juice

2 teaspoons curry
powder

1/2 teaspoon salt

1/4 teaspoon *each*
freshly ground
pepper and thyme

2 cups pitted prunes,
quartered

1 tart green apple,
thinly sliced

1/3 cup dark raisins

3&1/2 pounds boned,
skinned chicken
breasts

1/2 cup *each* peanuts
and shredded
sweetened coconut

In large frying pan, heat oil over medium-high heat. Add onions and garlic and cook 6 to 8 minutes, or until they brown, stirring often. Add boiling water, lemon juice, spices, and fruits; stir until well blended. Add chicken to frying pan and cover pan tightly. Lower heat and simmer 30 minutes. Uncover pan, turn chicken pieces, recover, and simmer an additional 15 minutes. Transfer chicken to heated serving platter and garnish with peanuts and coconut. Spoon pan sauces over chicken.

North African Stew

Take an exotic trip with this recipe.
8 servings

Salt and freshly
  ground pepper
1/4 cup cumin
6 pounds chicken, cut
  into serving pieces
2&2/3 cups pitted
  prunes
1/4 cup chopped dates
1/2 cup raisins
1&1/2 tablespoons
  cinnamon
6 tablespoons olive oil
4 large Spanish or
  yellow onions,
  sliced
2 teaspoons turmeric
1 tablespoon ground
  ginger
Couscous
1 cup whole, un-
  blanched almonds,
  toasted

Combine salt, pepper, and cumin in small cup and sprinkle over chicken pieces. Set aside. In medium saucepan, combine fruits with cinnamon and cover with water. Bring to boil; remove from heat. Set aside. In large skillet, heat 3 tablespoons oil and sauté onions with turmeric and ginger, stirring frequently. Do not allow onions to brown. Remove from heat.

In Dutch oven, over moderate heat, add 3 tablespoons oil. Add chicken and brown lightly. Add onion mixture. Drain the fruit, reserving liquid. Add 1/2 cup fruit liquid to chicken and onion mixture. Bring to a boil, cover, and simmer for 25 minutes. Add fruit to Dutch oven and continue cooking for 15 minutes. If mixture becomes too dry, add more fruit liquid.

Prepare couscous according to package directions. Spread couscous on serving platter and top with chicken. Pour sauce over top to cover, putting any remainder in serving bowl. Sprinkle with toasted almonds.

SAUTÉED CHICKEN WITH PRUNES

Serve this chicken with hot buttered noodles and minted carrots.
8 servings

1/4 cup oil

2 chickens (3 pounds each), cut into serving pieces

1/2 cup (1 stick) butter

6 shallots, peeled and chopped

6 garlic cloves, minced

6 cups (1&1/2 750 ml. bottles) dry red wine

1 cup water

3 tablespoons flour

1/3 cup sugar

2&2/3 cups pitted prunes

In Dutch oven over moderately high heat, heat half of the oil. Add half of the chicken pieces and cook 15 minutes or until brown on all sides. Remove chicken to large broiler pan and set aside. Add remaining oil to pan and cook the remaining chicken. Add to same broiler pan. In same Dutch oven, melt butter over medium heat. Add shallots and garlic and cook 2 minutes or until shallots are soft, stirring occasionally. Add 4 cups of the wine and bring to a rolling boil, scraping brown bits from bottom of pan. Add water and boil wine mixture 20 minutes or until reduced to 3 cups. Set aside.

Preheat broiler.

Dust chicken pieces with flour and put under broiler 6 to 8 minutes or until flour browns slightly. Place chicken in a casserole and pour reduced wine over it. Cover and cook chicken over moderately low heat for 20 minutes or until chicken is done.

While chicken is cooking, heat the remaining 2 cups of wine and sugar in a 2-quart saucepan over moderately high heat. Stir until sugar dissolves. Add prunes to saucepan. Reduce heat slightly, cover pan, and simmer 20 minutes.

Remove prunes and wine to work bowl of a food processor or blender and purée.

To serve, put buttered noodles on platter, spread with puréed prunes and nest chicken pieces on top. Ladle sauce from casserole over chicken.

TANGY CHICKEN

8 servings

Preheat oven to 350°.

1 jar (8 ounces)
   apricot preserves
1 envelope (1&1/4
   ounces) onion soup
1 bottle (8 ounces)
   French dressing
1 small jar prune
   puree (baby food)
2 chickens, cut into
   serving pieces

In small bowl, combine first 4 ingredients.

Place chicken in large baking dish. Spread sauce over chicken. Bake for 1&1/2 hours. You can refrigerate any remaining sauce and use it within a week as a glaze for spareribs.

Roast Duck with Ruby Prune Sauce

Duck is special anytime, especially with this ruby sauce. Serve with wild rice and a spinach salad.
4 servings

2 cups pitted prunes
1 4-pound duck
1 garlic clove
1 tart green apple,
    quartered

Ruby Prune Sauce:
1 tablespoon butter
1 teaspoon minced
    garlic
1 teaspoon fresh
    lemon juice
Freshly ground white
    pepper
1 teaspoon tomato
    paste
2 teaspoons corn-
    starch
1 cup chicken stock
2 teaspoons red
    currant jelly
1 bay leaf

2 tablespoons finely
    chopped chives for
    garnish

Put prunes in small saucepan; cover with water. Bring to boil and simmer 12 minutes. Drain prunes, reserving cooking liquid.

Preheat oven to 300°.

Dry duck inside and out with paper towel. Place garlic clove, 6 drained prunes, and apple in cavity. Tie or truss the duck. Prick skin all over and insert meat thermometer in thickest part of thigh. Put duck on rack in roasting pan and cook for about 1&1/2 hours or until meat thermometer registers 180°. While duck is baking, make sauce.

To make ruby prune sauce: In medium sauce-pan, melt butter over low heat. Add minced garlic and cook for 1 minute. Remove from heat. Add lemon juice, pepper, tomato paste, and cornstarch. Add stock and 3/4 cup cooking liquid reserved from prunes, stirring well. Cook over medium heat, stirring constantly until mixture boils. Add jelly and bay leaf, reduce heat to low; simmer for 15 minutes. Remove bay leaf and add reserved prunes.

CONTINUED

When duck is ready to be served, remove and discard prunes and apple from cavity. Carve into serving pieces and place on warmed platter. With slotted spoon, remove prunes from sauce and arrange around duck. Spoon sauce over duck and sprinkle with chives. Serve any remaining sauce on the side.

GAME

Rabbit Stew with Mushrooms

This unusual stew is sure to delight your friends.
8 servings

Marinade:

1/4 cup olive oil

2/3 cup red wine vinegar

2 garlic cloves, minced

1 large onion, thinly sliced

1 tablespoon *each* peppercorns and juniper berries

1 bay leaf, crumbled

1 teaspoon thyme

—

2 2&1/2- to 3-pound rabbits, fresh or frozen, cut up

9 tablespoons olive oil

20 pearl onions, peeled

3 carrots, cut into discs 2 inches thick

2 garlic cloves, minced

1&1/2 pounds new red potatoes, halved

In large glass bowl, combine all marinade ingredients. Stir rabbit pieces in marinade and coat evenly. Cover bowl and refrigerate 24 hours, turning rabbit pieces occasionally. Allow the rabbit to come to room temperature before cooking.

In large skillet, heat 3 tablespoons of the oil over moderately low heat. Sauté onions and carrots for 5 minutes, then add 2 garlic cloves. Transfer this mixture to large casserole.

Remove rabbit from marinade and discard marinade. Add 4 tablespoons of the oil to same skillet; over moderately high heat, brown rabbit pieces, a few at a time, adding more oil as needed. Transfer browned rabbit to casserole with onions and carrots. Add potatoes. Set aside. In small saucepan over high heat, reduce wine to 2 cups. Blend mustard and stock into wine and set aside.

Preheat oven to 325°.

You should have 3 tablespoons oil in skillet. If not, add oil to equal that amount. Remove skillet from heat and add flour to make a paste. Over moderately low heat, return skillet and

CONTINUED

3 cups dry red wine

1 tablespoon Dijon
   mustard

1 cup chicken stock

3 tablespoons flour

1 bay leaf

Salt and freshly
   ground pepper

1 cup pitted prunes

2 tablespoons butter

2 cups mushrooms,
   sliced

1 tablespoon chopped
   parsley

cook flour and oil until browned. Add reduced wine mixture and bring to a boil, stirring constantly with a wire whisk. Lower heat and simmer 5 minutes until sauce is smooth. Pour sauce over rabbit in casserole. Add bay leaf, salt, and pepper. Cover and bake in oven for 30 minutes, basting with sauce occasionally. Remove casserole from oven and add prunes. Replace cover, return casserole to oven, and bake another 30 minutes or until rabbit is tender.

Fifteen minutes before rabbit is done, heat remaining 2 tablespoons of the oil and 2 tablespoons butter in large skillet over moderately high heat. When foam subsides, add mushrooms and sauté them for 10 minutes. Add to casserole. Remove bay leaf from sauce and discard. Add salt and pepper if needed and sprinkle with chopped parsley.

Note: Frozen rabbit should defrost 2 days in the refrigerator before marinating it.

VEGETARIAN

CURRY CORNUCOPIA

1 large (1 pound)
  eggplant, peeled,
  in 1-inch cubes
1/2 teaspoon salt
2 tablespoons oil
2 teaspoons oil
2 tablespoons curry
  powder
1&1/2 teaspoons cumin
2 garlic cloves, minced
2 large onions, cut into
  1-inch pieces
1 cup pitted prunes,
  quartered
3/4 cup water
2 medium carrots,
  sliced in 1/4-inch
  pieces
1 large potato, cubed
1 small cauliflower, cut
  in bite-size pieces
1 medium summer
  squash, halved, in
  1/2 inch discs
1 can (16 ounces)
  chickpeas, drained
1/4 cup raisins
1/2 cup prune juice
1/4 cup water
1/2 teaspoon cinnamon
Salt and pepper
Yogurt for garnish

Golden curry filled with vegetables and fruit. Serve on a bed of rice.
8 servings

Sprinkle eggplant with salt and drain in colander for 15 minutes. Pat dry with paper towel.

In large Dutch oven, heat 2 tablespoons oil over medium heat. Add eggplant, and cook approximately 5 minutes, stirring frequently. Remove eggplant with slotted spoon and set aside. In same pan, place 2 teaspoons oil and heat. Add curry powder, cumin, garlic, and onions. Sauté over medium heat 2 minutes, stirring often. Add prunes and 3/4 cup water. Bring to a simmer and add carrots, potato, cauliflower, and squash. Cover and simmer 7 minutes. Add reserved eggplant, chickpeas, raisins, prune juice, and water. Stir in cinnamon and salt and pepper to taste. Cover and cook over medium heat until vegetables are tender, about 10 minutes. Serve hot or cold with dollop of yogurt on top.

PRUNE NUT LOAF

Serve this versatile dish by itself as an entrée or coupled with a salad and stuffed in pita bread.
4 to 6 servings

Preheat oven to 350°.

1/2 cup walnuts, finely ground

1/4 cup *each* almonds and cashews, finely ground

3/4 cup wheat germ

1/4 cup oat bran

1 cup grated mild cheddar cheese

3/4 cup prune juice

3 eggs, well beaten

1 large onion, finely chopped

1 teaspoon thyme

1/2 teaspoon *each* marjoram and salt

In large bowl, mix all ingredients together until well blended. Turn into a greased 9 x 5-inch loaf pan. Bake for 45 minutes or until firm. Allow to cool slightly and turn out on serving platter.

South-of-the-Border Pie

The construction crew that was rebuilding the back porch the day we tested this recipe voted this their favorite.
6 servings

Preheat oven to 350°.

Filling:

1 can (16 ounces) kidney beans, drained

1/2 cup pitted prunes

2 tablespoons oil

1/4 cup chopped onion

1/2 teaspoon garlic powder

2 teaspoons chili powder

3/4 teaspoon salt

1/2 cup canned corn, drained

Topping:

2&1/2 cups cold water

1&1/2 cups yellow cornmeal

1 teaspoon salt

1/2 teaspoon chili powder

1/2 cup grated cheddar cheese

In work bowl of food processor, puree beans and prunes. In skillet, add oil and sauté onions until translucent. Add remaining filling ingredients and cook, stirring frequently, over medium heat for 3 to 4 minutes. Set aside.

Combine all topping ingredients, except cheese, in saucepan. Cook over medium heat until cornmeal thickens and begins to boil, stirring constantly.

Grease an 8-inch pie pan and spread with filling. Cover with topping and sprinkle with cheese. Bake uncovered for 30 minutes.

SPINACH KUGEL WITH GREEN PASTA

Kugel is a traditional Jewish dish. Serve this kugel with homemade apple sauce on the side.
4 servings

Preheat oven to 350°.

1 10-ounce package frozen, chopped spinach

1/2 cup Neufchâtel cheese

1 cup low-fat, small-curd cottage cheese

3 eggs

1&1/4 cups milk

1/2 cup *each* pitted prunes, cut into raisin-size pieces, and raisins

1/2 teaspoon *each* cinnamon and salt

4 ounces dry, green fettucini

Cook spinach according to package directions. Drain spinach and set aside.

In large mixing bowl, combine Neufchâtel cheese, cottage cheese, and eggs. Add milk, prunes, raisins, cinnamon, and salt and blend well. Set aside.

In large saucepan, boil fettucini according to package directions. Drain. Add spinach and fettucini to cheese mixture, combining thoroughly. Pour mixture into a buttered 1&1/2 quart baking dish and bake for 1 hour or until firm.

SURPRISE SOUFFLÉ

This casserole has a light soufflélike topping and a dense bottom rich with carrots and prunes.
4 servings

Preheat oven to 350°.

1 pound carrots,
   grated
1/2 cup pitted prunes,
   pureed
1 cup prune juice
2 tablespoons (1/4
   stick) butter
2 tablespoons chopped
   parsley
1 teaspoon soy sauce

Topping:
2 tablespoons (1/4
   stick) butter
2 tablespoons flour
1/2 cup milk
3 eggs, beaten
3/4 cup grated
   cheddar cheese

In saucepan, combine carrots, prunes, prune juice, and butter. Cover and simmer 15 minutes or until carrots are tender. In work bowl of food processor, puree carrot mixture, parsley, and soy sauce until smooth. Spread mixture in bottom of greased 1-quart soufflé dish.

To make topping: Melt butter in small saucepan. Add flour and cook 1 minute. Stir in milk and continue simmering for 2 minutes or until thickened. Remove pan from heat, add eggs and cheese, and stir to blend. Pour topping over carrot mixture and bake for 45 minutes or until topping is set.

Sweet-and-Sour Vegetable Tofu

These tangy, crunchy vegetables served with brown rice provide a delicious, complete meal.
4 to 6 servings

3/4 cup pineapple juice reserved from canned pineapple chunks (add water to complete measure if necessary)

1/3 cup rice vinegar

2 tablespoons soy sauce

1/2 cup pitted prunes, pureed

2 tablespoons cornstarch

2 tablespoons honey

2 teaspoons minced fresh ginger

2 tablespoons safflower oil

2 large carrots, thinly sliced

2 red bell peppers, sliced

1 large onion, sliced

1 garlic clove, minced

3/4 pound tofu, drained and cut into 1/2-inch cubes

1 cup pineapple chunks, drained and reserved

In nonmetallic bowl, whisk together the first 7 ingredients. Set aside. In large skillet, heat oil over high heat and stir-fry carrots, peppers, onion, and garlic for 3 minutes. Add reserved pineapple juice mixture and cook and stir until sauce thickens. Fold in tofu and pineapple chunks. Heat through. Serve on hot rice.

Note: Tofu is a common Asian food made from soybeans. Low in fat and high in protein, it is an excellent substitute for meat.

ACCOMPANIMENTS

AUTUMN PILAF

You can enjoy this rice dish as a vegetarian main course or as an accompaniment to your favorite chicken dish.
4 servings

3 tablespoons currants
1/4 cup *each* pitted prunes and dried apricots, cut into narrow strips
1/4 cup (1/2 stick) butter
1/4 cup pine nuts *or* unsalted cashews
1 tablespoon honey
1 cup uncooked long-grain white rice
2 cups chicken broth

Soak fruits in bowl of warm water to cover for 7 minutes. Drain. Melt butter in large saucepan over medium-high heat. Add fruits and nuts. Reduce heat to low and cook uncovered for 5 minutes, or until the nuts are lightly browned. Stir in the honey and rice, cover with chicken broth, and bring to a boil over high heat. Reduce the heat to low, cover the pan, and simmer 25 minutes, or until all of the liquid has been absorbed. Serve hot.

Note: You can substitute brown rice for white rice. Follow directions on package for time and add additional chicken broth if more is needed.

CALIFORNIA HARVEST STUFFING

Rich and fruity, this is sure to become a family favorite.
About 6 cups

1/2 cup (1 stick) butter
1 cup sliced onions
1 cup pitted prunes, chopped
1/2 cup *each* dried apricots and walnuts, chopped
1/4 cup chopped parsley
1 tablespoon herb of your choice (sage, thyme, marjoram, crushed rosemary)
3/4 cup chicken broth
1/2 cup dry sherry
1 package (8 ounces) corn-bread stuffing mix
Salt and freshly ground pepper

In Dutch oven, melt butter. Add onions, prunes, apricots, walnuts, parsley, and herb. Cook and stir until onions are limp. Add broth and sherry. Cover and simmer 5 minutes. Stir in stuffing mix to moisten. Cover; let stand 5 minutes. Season with salt and pepper. Serve as a side dish.

CURRIED PILAF

Adds interest to pork, lamb, or duck and is especially good with grilled kebabs.
4 to 5 servings

1/2 cup *each* pitted prunes and dried apricots
2 tablespoons golden raisins
2 tablespoons (1/4 stick) butter
1 small onion, chopped
1 tablespoon curry powder
1/2 teaspoon ground cumin
1 tablespoon tomato paste
1&1/2 cups uncooked long-grain white rice
3 cups chicken stock, heated
Salt and freshly ground pepper

Place prunes and apricots in small saucepan and cover with water. Bring to a boil and simmer until tender, about 10 minutes. Drain and cut into pieces. Reserve. Place raisins in cup; cover with hot water. Allow to sit for 3 minutes. Drain and add to prune and apricot pieces.

In heavy saucepan, melt butter, add onion, and cook over low heat until soft. Add curry, cumin, and tomato paste. Cook 1 minute, stirring frequently. Add rice and blend with curry mixture. Add hot stock and bring to a boil. Reduce heat, cover, and simmer for 25 to 30 minutes. Add salt and pepper to taste. Add fruit to rice and stir gently to mix. Serve immediately.

FESTIVE NOODLE KUGEL

This traditional Jewish dish is often served for family get-togethers at holiday time. Using a nondairy margarine, you can serve this kugel with meat to people who adhere to the kosher dietary laws.

6 to 8 servings

Crust:

1/4 cup (1/2 stick) margarine, melted
1/2 cup brown sugar
1 cup pecans, coarsely chopped

Noodle Mixture:

1 package (8 ounces) 1/2-inch wide noodles
2 tablespoons margarine, melted
2 eggs
1/4 cup raisins
8 dried apricots, coarsely chopped
4 pitted prunes, coarsely chopped
1 apple, cored and thinly sliced
1/4 cup sugar
1/4 teaspoon *each* cinnamon and salt

Topping:

1/4 cup cornflakes, coarsely crushed
2 tablespoons (1/4 stick) margarine, softened

To make crust: Mix together margarine, brown sugar, and pecans. Spread on bottom of 7 x 11-inch glass baking pan.

To make noodle mixture: Boil noodles according to package directions. Drain. In mixing bowl, toss noodles with melted margarine. Combine with remaining ingredients and mix well. Refrigerate about 2 hours and then pour over prepared crust.

Preheat oven to 350°.

To make topping: Mix together cornflake crumbs and margarine. Sprinkle on top of noodle mixture. Bake for 1&1/2 hours. Serve hot.

HARVEST STUFFING

California prunes and pears are the intriguing ingredients in this savory stuffing perfect with chicken, turkey, or pork.
6 cups

Preheat oven to 350°.

2 cups pitted prunes, coarsely chopped

1/2 cup hot chicken bouillon or water

1/2 cup (1 stick) butter

1 cup *each* chopped celery and onions

1&1/2 cups diced pears

6 cups lightly packed bread cubes

1 teaspoon *each* salt and thyme

1/2 teaspoon freshly ground pepper

1/4 teaspoon allspice

In small bowl, combine prunes and bouillon; set aside. Melt butter in Dutch oven. Stir in celery and onions. Cook over medium heat 5 minutes. Stir in pears. Cook 2 minutes. Add bread, prune mixture, and seasonings; cook and stir 2 minutes. Use to stuff chicken or turkey or spoon into buttered 1&1/2-quart casserole. Cover and bake for 30 minutes or until heated through.

LENTILS IN CURRIED VINAIGRETTE SALAD

This salad requires a sitting time of 24 hours. The results are well worth waiting for.
8 to 10 servings

2 cups dried red
   lentils

Vinaigrette:
3/4 cup corn oil
1/2 cup red wine
   vinegar
2 tablespoons curry
   powder
1 teaspoon sugar
1/2 teaspoon *each* salt
   and freshly ground
   pepper

1 cup pitted prunes,
   chopped
1/2 cup golden raisins
1/4 cup pitted dates,
   chopped
1 medium red onion,
   chopped

Rinse lentils in colander. Transfer lentils into quart of boiling water and boil 5 minutes. Rinse and drain well. Set aside.

In work bowl of food processor with metal blade inserted, process vinaigrette ingredients with 8 on-off pulses or until well blended.

Combine lentils with fruits and onion. Add 3/4 cup of vinaigrette and mix well. Refrigerate for 24 hours. Two hours before serving, add remaining vinaigrette if necessary. Serve on bed of fresh spinach and garnish with cherry tomatoes. Extra vinaigrette may be served on the side.

MEDITERRANEAN PILAF

A superb accompaniment for a chicken or pork shish kebab.
4 to 6 servings

Pilaf:

2 tablespoons
  (1/4 stick) butter
1/3 cup chopped
  onion
1&1/2 cups uncooked
  long-grain white
  rice
3 cups chicken broth
  (homemade or
  canned)

**Fruit-Almond
  Mixture:**

2&1/2 tablespoons
  butter
3/4 cup *each* dried
  apricots and pitted
  prunes, quartered
3/4 cup raisins
1 tablespoon sugar or
  to taste
1/4 teaspoon cinna-
  mon
1/2 cup blanched
  almonds, slivered
  and toasted

To make pilaf: Melt 2 tablespoons butter in large frying pan over medium-high heat. Sauté onion until translucent. Add rice and sauté until golden. Add chicken broth, bring to a boil, cover tightly, and simmer over low heat for 25 minutes.

To make fruit-almond mixture: While rice is cooking, melt butter in large skillet over medium heat. Add fruits and stir until evenly coated. Sprinkle with sugar and cook gently, stirring frequently until thoroughly heated. Add cinnamon, almonds, and rice; mix gently.

PRUNE AND RICE TZIMMES

This easy dish will add an ethnic flair to any dinner.
6 to 8 servings

1 cup pitted prunes
1 quart hot water
1 cup uncooked long-
grain white rice
1/2 cup honey *or*
light-brown sugar
Juice and grated peel
of 1 lemon
1/2 cup (1 stick)
butter
1/4 teaspoon cinna-
mon
Pinch of salt

In heavy cooking pot, soak prunes for 30 minutes in water. Add rice and bring to a boil. Reduce heat; add remaining ingredients and simmer 30 minutes. Brown under broiler for a few minutes.

Stuffed Acorn Squash

Autumn is the peak season for apples and acorn squash. Take advantage of nature's bounties and enjoy this colorful and tasty dish.
4 servings

Preheat oven to 350°.

2 medium-size acorn squash, halved with seeds and pulp removed

1 tablespoon butter

1 tart green apple, peeled and chopped

1/3 cup pitted prunes, chopped

2 tablespoons raisins

1/2 cup onion, chopped

1 cup cooked brown rice

1 tablespoon lemon juice

1/4 teaspoon cinnamon

Place acorn squash halves cut side down on greased baking sheet. Bake for 30 minutes. Remove from oven and set aside.

Melt butter in medium skillet and add fruits and onion; cook 5 minutes. Add rice, lemon juice, and cinnamon and combine well. Stuff cooled squash halves with rice mixture and bake, covered, for 20 minutes.

TRADITIONAL SWEET POTATO TZIMMES

Handed down from one generation to the next, this specialty is served on Rosh Hashanah, the Jewish New Year. We found this recipe to be a welcome addition to festive family gatherings.
4 to 6 servings

1&1/3 cups pitted
prunes

4 large sweet potatoes,
peeled and cubed

1/4 cup brown sugar

1 pound carrots,
thinly sliced

1 can (12 ounces)
frozen orange juice
concentrate

1 juice can of water

Place all ingredients in large pot and cover. Cook over low heat until carrots are tender, approximately 1&1/2 to 2 hours. Transfer to warmed serving bowl and begin your own tradition.

COMPOTES

BON BON FRUIT COMPOTE

A heavenly fruit compote with an intensely rich flavor makes an easy, elegant company dessert.
6 servings (about 3 cups)

1&1/2 cups *each* prune juice and pitted prunes

1 cup dried apricot halves

1/2 cup golden raisins

1/2 cup water

2 tablespoons brandy *or* 2 teaspoons vanilla

Sweetened whipped cream

Semisweet chocolate curls *or* grated semisweet chocolate

In 2-quart saucepan, combine prune juice, fruits, and water. Bring to boil; reduce heat and simmer 10 minutes, stirring occasionally. Remove from heat; stir in brandy. Cool to lukewarm. Spoon into stemmed dessert glasses. Dollop with whipped cream and garnish with chocolate. If you wish, cover fruit and refrigerate; serve chilled.

Serving tip: Use this fruit mixture as a topping for vanilla or chocolate ice cream, pound cake, angel food cake, custard, rice pudding, or bread pudding.

Citrus Fruit Compote

This attractive compote enhances ham, pork, or lamb.
4 servings

1/2 cup pitted prunes

2 large oranges, peeled, seeded, and thinly sliced crosswise

2 small pink grape-fruits, peeled, seeded and thinly sliced crosswise

1/4 cup orange liqueur

1 teaspoon fresh orange juice

3 tablespoons sugar

Combine fruits and orange liqueur in large nonmetallic bowl. Cover and let stand over-night. Just before serving, add orange juice and stir to blend. Remove fruits with slotted spoon and arrange in oval broiler-proof serving dish. Pour juices over fruit and sprinkle with sugar. Broil until fruit just begins to brown.

DRIED FRUIT COMPOTE

Rated excellent by all. Dress up your next buffet.
8 servings

1/2 cup dried apples
1 cup *each* pitted
prunes and dried
apricots
1 can (6 ounces)
frozen white grape
juice concentrate
2 cups water
2 whole cloves
1 cinnamon stick
1/4 teaspoon whole
allspice
1 tablespoon lemon
juice
3 medium-size tart
green apples, peeled
and thinly sliced

Place dried fruits, juice, water, and spices in medium-size saucepan. Bring to a boil, cover, and simmer 20 minutes. Remove fruits with slotted spoon to serving bowl. To remaining juice in saucepan, add lemon juice and apples. Cover and simmer 5 minutes. Remove apples with slotted spoon and add to fruit in serving bowl, combining well. Strain juice to remove spices. Add to fruit; stir. Serve at room temperature or chilled.

Fuzzy Navel Compote

A Fuzzy Navel, a drink popular at brunches, is made with peach schnapps and orange juice. We like the combination so much, we created a compote using the same ingredients.
8 servings

2&2/3 cups pitted
 prunes
1/4 cup sugar
3 cups orange juice
1&1/2 cups dried
 peaches
2 navel oranges,
 peeled and thinly
 sliced crosswise
1/4 cup peach
 schnapps

Place prunes, sugar, and orange juice in medium-size saucepan. Bring to a boil, reduce heat, and simmer 10 minutes. Add peaches and oranges and cook an additional 5 minutes. Transfer fruit with slotted spoon to a serving bowl, reserving orange juice in pan. Bring juice to boil and reduce to 1&1/2 cups. Cool to room temperature. Stir in peach schnapps and combine with fruit in serving bowl. Serve at room temperature or chilled.

PRUNE CITRUS BOWL

Perfect partners in flavor and color, prunes and citrus help you "rise 'n' shine" in the morning.
6 servings

1&1/2 cups pitted prunes
3/4 cup orange juice
1/3 cup water
2 tablespoons honey
2 teaspoons grated fresh ginger
1 teaspoon grated orange peel
3 grapefruits
2 oranges
Mint sprigs for garnish

In 2-quart saucepan, combine prunes, orange juice, and water. Bring to a boil; remove from heat. Stir in honey, ginger, and orange peel. Cool; cover and chill. Halve grapefruits crosswise and carefully scoop sections into bowl. Pull out and discard membranes, being careful not to puncture shells. Rinse, drain, and reserve shells. Peel and section oranges. Combine citrus fruits with chilled prune mixture. Cover and chill. For each serving, portion equally into grapefruit shells. Garnish with mint.

Note: If fresh ginger is unavailable, substitute 4 teaspoons ground ginger; stir into prunes, orange juice, and water before bringing to a boil.

PRUNES IN BURGUNDY

Looks lovely in a glass bowl for a brunch and makes a nice light dessert after a hearty meal.
10 servings

1 cup water
1/2 cup sugar
8 whole allspice
10 whole cloves
3 cinnamon sticks
10 slivers of orange
  peel
1 bottle (750 ml.)
  burgundy
2&2/3 cups pitted
  prunes

In large saucepan, combine water, sugar, spices, and orange peel. Bring to a boil and continue boiling until liquid is syrupy, approximately 10 minutes. Add burgundy and prunes, reduce heat, and simmer 20 minutes. Transfer prunes with a slotted spoon to a glass bowl. Strain liquid, discard spices, and pour over prunes. Serve at room temperature.

Note: This recipe improves with age. You can refrigerate it for 3 to 4 weeks.

RUBYFRUIT PRUNE COMPOTE

The tangy flavor of prunes is spiked with the rich spirit of port in this elegant dish. Try it over vanilla ice cream or as an accompaniment to pork or poultry.
6 servings

2 cups pitted prunes

1&1/3 cups Calimyrna figs

1&1/2 cups ruby port

3/4 cup water

2 tablespoons honey

2 teaspoons lemon juice

3 navel oranges, peeled and cut into segments

Rosemary sprigs for garnish (optional)

In 2- to 3-quart saucepan, combine prunes, figs, port, water, and honey. Bring to a boil, reduce heat, and simmer until fruits are tender but not soft, about 10 minutes. Remove fruits to bowl with slotted spoon. Bring liquid in saucepan to boil over medium-high heat. Cook about 5 minutes until reduced by one third. Remove from heat; stir in lemon juice, then pour over fruits. Cool, cover, and chill. To serve, spoon fruits with their liquid and the orange segments into dessert dishes. Garnish with rosemary, if you wish, when serving compote with a meat or poultry entrée.

Note: You can store this compote in the refrigerator for up to 2 weeks.

SIMMERING FRUIT POTPOURRI
6 servings

2 cups apple juice
1/2 cup dark-brown
  sugar
1/2 teaspoon *each*
  lemon juice and
  vanilla
1/4 teaspoon *each*
  ground ginger and
  nutmeg
1/2 teaspoon cinna-
  mon
3 cups mixed dried
  fruits

Combine all ingredients in large saucepan over moderate heat. Cover and simmer 15 minutes or until fruit is tender. Serve warm.

BREADS

MUFFINS

AFTER-SCHOOL MUFFINS

These muffins are a favorite after-school snack. After all, who can resist chocolate chips?
12 muffins

Preheat oven to 350°.

1/2 cup (1 stick) butter, room temperature

1/2 cup light-brown sugar

1/2 cup sugar

2 teaspoons vanilla

2 eggs

1/2 cup pureed prunes

2/3 cup milk

1&3/4 cups flour

1/2 teaspoon salt

1 tablespoon baking powder

1/4 cup unprocessed bran (not cereal)

3/4 cup milk-chocolate chips

1 cup walnuts, coarsely chopped

In large bowl, cream butter, sugars, and vanilla. Add eggs, pureed prunes, and milk, beating well. In small bowl, combine flour, salt, baking powder, and bran. Add dry ingredients to batter, stirring just until moistened. Carefully fold in chocolate chips and walnuts. Spoon into greased muffin tins, filling each cup two thirds full. Bake for 20 to 25 minutes. Cool 5 minutes then remove to wire racks. Serve with a large glass of milk and enjoy!

Banana-Prune Crunchy Muffins

A delicious way to add nutrition to any meal.
12 muffins

Preheat oven to 400°.

1 cup flour

2/3 cup whole-wheat
flour

1/4 cup wheat germ

1&1/2 cups granola

1/4 cup light-brown
sugar

1 tablespoon baking
powder

1/2 teaspoon *each*
baking soda and salt

1/2 cup milk

1/2 cup stewed, pitted
prunes, drained and
quartered

2 medium-size
bananas, mashed

1/3 cup butter, melted

1 egg, lightly beaten

Topping:

3/4 cup powdered
sugar

4 to 5 teaspoons
orange juice

1 teaspoon grated
orange peel

In large mixing bowl, combine dry ingredients. Add milk, prunes, bananas, butter, and egg. Stir with a wooden spoon until just moistened (batter may be lumpy). Fill greased muffin tins two thirds full and bake for 20 minutes or until muffins are golden brown. While muffins are cooling, mix together topping ingredients in small bowl. Drizzle topping over muffins while they are still warm.

BUTTERMILK-PRUNE MUFFINS

*These muffins are a breakfast delight especially
when topped with Prune Apple Butter (page
223).*
12 muffins

Preheat oven to 400°.

1 cup pitted prunes

5 tablespoons butter,
room temperature

3 tablespoons sugar

2 eggs, well beaten

1 cup buttermilk,
room temperature

1/2 teaspoon *each* salt,
nutmeg, and baking
soda

1/4 teaspoon cinna-
mon

3 cups bread flour,
sifted

1 tablespoon baking
powder

1/2 cup walnuts, finely
chopped

In small saucepan, bring 2 cups water to boil.
Drop prunes into boiling water and let sit 7
minutes. Drain prunes and cut into fine pieces
with kitchen shears. Set aside.

In large mixing bowl, cream butter until light
and fluffy. Gradually add sugar and beat until
well blended. Add beaten eggs and buttermilk.

Put dry ingredients in sifter and sift over prune
pieces. Toss to coat. Add flour mix, prunes, and
walnuts to batter and stir just to incorporate
ingredients. Pour into greased muffin tins; bake
for 25 minutes or until muffins pull away from
sides of pan.

DOUBLE-FRUIT BRAN MUFFINS

With a food processor, you can quickly prepare these muffins as part of a healthy breakfast.
12 muffins

Preheat oven to 375°.

1&1/3 cups All-Bran cereal
1/2 cup pitted prunes
1/4 cup *each* dates and walnuts
1 cup flour
2 teaspoons baking powder
1/2 teaspoon baking soda
1/4 teaspoon salt
1/2 cup sugar
3/4 cup buttermilk
1/4 cup oil
2 large eggs
1 teaspoon vanilla

In food processor or blender, process cereal until finely chopped, about 30 seconds. Add prunes, dates, and walnuts and process 5 seconds. Add remaining ingredients to processor bowl and process for 3 seconds. Scrape down the sides of the bowl and process again for 2 seconds.

Fill greased muffin cups two thirds full with batter. Bake for 23 to 25 minutes or until the muffins are golden brown and firm to the touch. Cool in pan for about 10 minutes. Serve while still warm.

GLAZED MARMALADE MUFFINS

Like cupcakes, these muffins have their own sweet topping.
12 muffins

Preheat oven to 375°.

1&1/2 cups flour
2 teaspoons baking
powder
1/2 teaspoon *each* salt,
baking soda, and
cinnamon
1/4 teaspoon nutmeg
1/2 cup sugar
1/2 cup pitted prunes,
chopped
1 egg
1/2 cup sour cream
1/4 cup orange mar-
malade
1 teaspoon finely
grated orange peel
1/3 cup butter, melted
and barely warm

Glaze:
2 cups powdered
sugar
1/4 cup orange juice
1 teaspoon vanilla

Mix together dry ingredients and prunes in large mixing bowl. In separate bowl, beat egg. Stir sour cream, marmalade, orange peel, and melted butter into egg. Add egg mixture to dry ingredients and mix just to blend.

Spoon into well-greased muffin tins and bake for 15 to 20 minutes or until top is firm to touch. Remove to wire rack and let sit 5 to 10 minutes.

While muffins are baking, combine glaze ingredients in small bowl. After baking but while muffins are still warm, dip tops in glaze.

HIGH-FIBER PRUNE MUFFINS

This satisfying muffin, mellow sweet with prunes and crunchy with walnuts, is simple to prepare. Make a double batch and freeze half— always ready for a nutritious snack on the go.
12 muffins

Preheat oven to 425°.

1/2 cup unprocessed bran (not cereal)
1/2 cup *each* prune juice and milk
1/4 cup light-brown sugar
2 eggs, lightly beaten
1&1/2 cups flour
2 teaspoons baking powder
1 teaspoon nutmeg
1/2 teaspoon salt
1/4 cup (1/2 stick) melted butter
1 cup pitted prunes, coarsely chopped
1/2 cup walnuts, chopped

In large bowl, mix bran, prune juice, milk, and sugar; set aside 10 minutes. Stir in eggs, then flour, baking powder, nutmeg, and salt to blend thoroughly. Stir in butter, then prunes and walnuts. Spoon into greased muffin tins. Sprinkle with additional bran, if desired. Bake for 15 to 20 minutes until lightly browned and springy to the touch. Cool on rack.

PEANUT BUTTER MUFFINS

Peanut butter was created in 1890 by a physician concerned about his elderly patients who were toothless and unable to chew. Because peanuts are high in protein and easily digested, he thought this would be an excellent way to provide protein in their diet.
12 muffins

Preheat oven to 375°.

1&1/2 cups flour
1/2 cup sugar
2 teaspoons baking powder
1/2 teaspoon salt
1/2 cup chunky peanut butter
1/4 cup (1/2 stick) butter
1 cup milk
2 eggs, lightly beaten
1/2 cup pitted prunes, chopped and tossed with 1 teaspoon flour
Sugar

In large bowl, mix dry ingredients. With a pastry blender or fork, cut in peanut butter and butter until mixture is crumbly. Add remaining ingredients and stir just to blend. Spoon into greased muffin tins, filling two thirds full. Sprinkle tops with sugar and bake for 15 to 20 minutes.

PRUNE-PUMPKIN MUFFINS

4 eggs

2 cups sugar

1&1/2 cups oil

1 can (16 ounces) solid packed pumpkin

2&2/3 cups flour

1/3 cup unprocessed bran (not cereal)

1 tablespoon cinnamon

2 teaspoons *each* baking powder and baking soda

1 teaspoon salt

1/2 teaspoon nutmeg

1 cup *each* raisins and chopped prunes

1 teaspoon flour

Frosting:

1 package (8 ounces) cream cheese, softened

1/4 cup (1/2 stick) butter, room temperature

2 cups powdered sugar

1&1/2 teaspoons vanilla

1 tablespoon finely grated orange peel

A great new addition to Halloween fare.
24 muffins

Preheat oven to 375°.

In large bowl, beat eggs slightly. Add sugar, oil, and pumpkin. Blend well. Add dry ingredients and mix until smooth. Toss the raisins and prunes in the teaspoon of flour, and stir into batter. Fill greased muffin cups two thirds full and bake for 15 to 20 minutes.

To make frosting: While muffins are cooling, combine cream cheese and butter in large mixing bowl and beat until light and fluffy. Gradually add sugar. Beat until well blended. Mix in vanilla and orange rind. Spread on cooled muffins.

Rise 'n' Shine Breakfast Muffins

12 muffins

Preheat oven to 425°.

1/2 cup plus 2 table-
spoons rolled oats
3/4 cup prune juice
1/4 cup milk
5 tablespoons light-
brown sugar
2 eggs, lightly beaten
1&1/2 cups flour
2 teaspoons baking
powder
1 teaspoon nutmeg
1/2 teaspoon salt
1/4 cup (1/2 stick)
melted butter
1 cup pitted prunes,
coarsely chopped
1/2 cup walnuts,
chopped

In large bowl, mix 1/2 cup of the oats, prune juice, milk, and 4 tablespoons of the sugar; set aside 10 minutes. Stir in the eggs, then the dry ingredients to blend thoroughly. Stir in butter, then the prunes and walnuts. Spoon into greased muffin tins. Sprinkle evenly with the remaining sugar and oats. Bake in lower third of oven for 15 to 20 minutes until lightly browned and springy to the touch. Cool on rack. Cooled muffins may be securely wrapped and frozen, if desired. Bring to room temperature before serving, or cover lightly with foil and place in 325° oven until heated through, about 10 minutes.

WESTWARD-HO MUFFINS

High in fiber, rich in vitamins and minerals. Start on the trail to healthy eating with these muffins.
24 muffins

1 cup pitted prunes

3 eggs

1/3 cup light-brown sugar

2/3 cup oil

1/4 cup molasses

2 cups unprocessed bran (not cereal)

1 cup grated carrots

1&1/2 cups whole-wheat flour

1/2 cup wheat germ

1 teaspoon *each* baking soda and salt

2 teaspoons *each* baking powder and cinnamon

1 tablespoon powdered milk

1/2 cup raisins

In small saucepan, over medium-high heat, stew prunes in 2 cups water for 10 minutes. Drain, reserving 1&1/2 cups liquid. (If necessary, add water to measure 1&1/2 cups.) Reserve. With food processor, puree prunes. Set aside.

Preheat oven to 375°.

In large bowl, beat eggs, sugar, oil, molasses, bran, carrots, pureed prunes, and reserved cooking liquid. Stir well.

In medium bowl, mix together remaining ingredients. Add all at once to egg mixture, mixing only until moistened. Spoon into greased muffin tins, filling two-thirds full. Bake for 20 to 25 minutes.

QUICK BREADS

DONNA'S PRUNE BREAD

A wonderful finish for a midwinter dinner.
1 loaf

3/4 cup pitted prunes,
  chopped
1/4 cup orange juice
2 eggs
6 tablespoons butter
  (3/4 stick), room
  temperature
1/3 cup honey
3/4 cup sour cream
1 teaspoon grated
  orange peel
1 teaspoon vanilla
1 cup flour
1/2 cup whole-wheat
  flour
1 teaspoon *each*
  baking powder,
  baking soda, and
  salt
2&1/4 teaspoons
  cinnamon
1/2 cup pecans,
  chopped

In small glass bowl, marinate prunes in orange juice for several hours. Puree with liquid and set aside.

Preheat oven to 325°.

In large mixing bowl of electric mixer, beat eggs until light. Add butter, honey, sour cream, orange peel, vanilla, and prunes. Mix well.

Combine dry ingredients and pecans and fold into the batter. Pour batter into greased and floured 9 x 5-inch loaf pan. Bake for approximately 55 minutes. This will produce a moist bread, almost like a pudding, that can be served with ice cream. Bake for another 35 minutes to produce a tea bread. The tea bread is done when bread springs back when lightly touched with fingertips. Cool in pan 10 minutes and then remove to wire rack to finish cooling.

GRAPE-NUT–PRUNE BREAD

In 1891, C. W. Post was a patient in a sanitarium in Battle Creek, Michigan, and living on a diet of nuts, grains, and caramel "coffee" made from bran, molasses, and burnt bread crusts. Post later decided to create his own coffee substitute, Postum Cereal food drink. In 1897, he created one of the first cold cereals. He called it Grape-Nuts for its nutlike flavor and because he mistakenly thought that grape sugar was produced when the wheat was baked.
1 loaf

2 cups skim milk, scalded

1/4 cup unprocessed bran (not cereal)

1 cup Grape-Nuts

1&1/2 teaspoons salt

3 cups flour

4 teaspoons baking powder

1/2 cup sugar

1 egg, well beaten

3 tablespoons butter, melted

1 tablespoon finely grated orange peel

1 cup pitted prunes, stewed and pureed

1/3 cup apple sauce

Preheat oven to 350°.

In large bowl, pour hot milk over bran and Grape-Nuts. Allow to cool. In medium-size bowl, stir together salt, flour, baking powder, and sugar. Add beaten egg and butter to Grape-Nut–milk mixture and stir well. Add dry ingredients to batter, stirring only enough to incorporate. Gently fold in orange peel, prunes, and apple sauce. Turn into lightly greased 9 x 5-inch loaf pan. Bake for 1 hour and 20 minutes. Remove from pan and cool on rack.

HEARTY PRUNE BREAD

Laced with the wholesome flavors of prunes, honey, wheat germ, and nuts, this bread is delicious anytime. For an extra treat, serve toasted with butter.
1 loaf

1&1/2 cups pitted prunes, coarsely chopped

1/3 cup apple juice

2 eggs

1/2 cup *each* honey and oil

2&1/4 cups flour

1/3 cup wheat germ

2 teaspoons *each* baking powder and baking soda

1 teaspoon salt

3 tablespoons sour cream *or* unflavored yogurt

2/3 cup nuts, coarsely chopped

1/3 cup sunflower seeds

Preheat oven to 325°.

In small bowl, combine prunes and juice; set aside. In large bowl, beat eggs, honey, and oil. Beat in flour, wheat germ, baking powder, baking soda, and salt. Then mix in sour cream and prune mixture. Stir in nuts and seeds. Turn into greased 9 x 5-inch loaf pan; smooth top. Bake for 1 hour and 10 minutes or until toothpick inserted in center comes out clean. Cool in pan 15 minutes. Wrap in aluminum foil while still warm.

Oat-Nut Bread

Dense and delicious.
1 loaf

Preheat oven to 350°.

1&1/2 cups flour
1&1/2 cups oat flour
(see method at
right)
1/2 cup dark-brown
sugar
2 teaspoons baking
powder
1/4 teaspoon *each*
mace and salt
1/2 teaspoon nutmeg
1&1/3 cups milk
1 egg, beaten
1/4 cup salad oil
1/2 cup *each* pitted
prunes and pecans,
chopped and
dredged with 1
tablespoon flour

In work bowl of food processor or blender, process enough rolled oats to produce 1&1/2 cups oat flour.

Combine dry ingredients in large mixing bowl. In medium-size bowl, stir together milk, egg, and oil. Gradually add dry ingredients to milk mixture. Stir in prunes and pecans. Spoon batter into greased 9 x 5-inch loaf pan and bake for 50 to 60 minutes or until top is brown and firm to the touch. Let bread cool on rack 10 minutes before removing from pan.

PRUNE-MOLASSES BREAD

This outstanding bread tastes like Boston brown bread.
1 cylindrical loaf

1/2 cup pitted prunes
1/4 cup raisins
1 cup unprocessed
  bran (not cereal)
1 cup buttermilk
1 tablespoon molasses
1/2 cup sugar
1 cup bread flour
1/2 teaspoon baking
  soda
1 teaspoon baking
  powder
1/4 teaspoon salt

Place prunes and raisins in small saucepan with enough water to cover. Bring to a boil and simmer 15 minutes. Drain. Puree fruits and set aside.

Combine bran, buttermilk, prunes, and molasses and blend well. Gradually add dry ingredients to prune mixture, combining thoroughly after each addition. Spoon into heavily greased 1-pound coffee can. Cover can top tightly with buttered aluminum foil. Place can in large, deep pot. Fill pot with 3 inches of hot water, cover pot, and steam for 3 hours over medium heat. You may need to add more water to pot. Remove aluminum foil and cool bread in can on wire rack. Cool bread completely before slicing. The flavor improves if you let the bread, wrapped in plastic wrap, stand overnight in a cool, dry place. Serve with cream cheese or Prune Butter (see page 224).

SUNSHINE TEA LOAF

1&1/4 cups flour

2 tablespoons wheat
germ

1 teaspoon *each*
baking powder and
baking soda

1/2 teaspoon salt

1&1/4 cups whole-
wheat flour

1/3 cup molasses

1/3 cup light-brown
sugar

1/4 cup oil

1&1/2 cups buttermilk

3/4 cup pitted prunes,
chopped and dredged
in 1 teaspoon flour

1 teaspoon finely grated
orange peel

**Cream-Cheese
Spread:**

2 packages (3 ounces
each) cream cheese,
room temperature

3 tablespoons butter,
room temperature

1&1/2 cups powdered
sugar

1 teaspoon vanilla

1&1/4 teaspoons finely
grated orange peel

This robust bread is chock-full of flavor. Serve it generously topped with cream-cheese spread.
1 loaf

Preheat oven to 375°.

In medium-size bowl, stir together first 6 ingredients. Set aside.

In large bowl of electric mixer, combine molasses, sugar, and oil. Beat at medium speed until well blended. Add flour mixture alternately with the buttermilk to the batter, beating well after each addition. Stir in prunes and orange peel. Pour batter into greased and floured 9 x 5-inch loaf pan. Bake for 50 to 55 minutes. Bread is done when tester in middle of loaf comes out clean. Cool 10 minutes in pan, then remove to wire rack to finish cooling.

To make cream-cheese spread: In small bowl, combine all ingredients. Blend until smooth and creamy. Serve loaf with spread. It's a great combination.

CARDAMOM-ORANGE COFFEE CAKE

Cardamom is an aromatic spice with a sweet, lemony flavor. In the Far East it is used to flavor coffee, the Scandinavians use it in their breads and pastries, and it is a standard ingredient in curry powder.
8-inch round cake

1 cup orange juice

Peel from 1 orange, finely grated

2 tablespoons (1/4 stick) butter

1 cup pitted prunes

2 cups flour

1/2 teaspoon salt

1 cup sugar

1 teaspoon baking powder

1/2 teaspoon baking soda

1&1/4 teaspoons cardamom

1 egg, lightly beaten

Glaze:

1 cup powdered sugar

2 tablespoons orange juice

1/2 teaspoon vanilla

Preheat oven to 350°.

Place orange juice, peel, butter, and prunes in a saucepan. Bring to a boil and simmer for 5 minutes. Remove pan from heat and let cool for 10 minutes. In work bowl of food processor or blender, puree prunes and liquid. Set aside.

In large mixing bowl, combine dry ingredients. Add pureed prune mixture and blend well. Beat in egg. Spoon batter into greased and floured 8-inch round pan. Bake for 40 to 45 minutes or until cake tester inserted in center of cake comes out clean. Cool in pan 10 minutes and then invert cake onto wire rack.

While cake is cooling, combine glaze ingredients in small bowl. Drizzle glaze over top of cake.

DOUBLE-FRUIT COFFEE CAKE

There are many recipes for sour cream coffee cake, but the addition of prunes and apricots makes this recipe unique.
1 cake

3/4 cup *each* pitted prunes and dried apricots, coarsely chopped

1 tablespoon flour

1/2 cup light-brown sugar

2 tablespoons (1/4 stick) butter, room temperature

2 tablespoons flour

1 teaspoon cinnamon

1/2 cup toasted pecans, chopped

3 cups flour

1&1/2 teaspoons baking powder

3/4 teaspoon baking soda

1/4 teaspoon salt

3/4 cup (1&1/2 sticks) butter, room temperature

1&1/2 cups sugar

4 eggs

1&1/2 teaspoons vanilla

1 cup sour cream

Preheat oven to 350°.

Place prunes and apricots in small bowl. Dust with 1 tablespoon flour and set aside.

Combine brown sugar, 2 tablespoons butter, 2 tablespoons flour, cinnamon, and pecans; mix with fork until crumbly.

Sift together 3 cups flour, baking powder, baking soda, and salt in bowl. In large mixing bowl, cream 3/4 cup butter until fluffy. Gradually add sugar, scraping down sides of bowl. Add eggs, one at a time, beating well after each addition. Continue beating until mixture is light and fluffy, about 3 to 5 minutes. Mix in vanilla. On low speed, alternately add flour mixture and sour cream, beginning and ending with flour. Beat until just smooth, about 1 minute. Carefully fold in prunes and apricots.

Spoon one third of batter into greased and floured 10-inch tube pan, spreading evenly. Crumble one third of brown-sugar mixture over batter. Repeat with remaining batter and brown sugar 2 more times. Bake for 1 hour and 15 minutes or until cake tester inserted in center comes out clean. Cool slightly and then turn cake out onto wire rack.

Glaze:

1 teaspoon vanilla

2 tablespoons hot
   milk

2 cups powdered
   sugar

To make glaze: While cake is cooling, mix vanilla and hot milk into powdered sugar. Very gradually, add more milk, a small amount at a time, until the glaze is the consistency of a thick cream sauce. Place cake on rack over a large piece of aluminum foil or waxed paper. Immediately pour glaze over cake and let it run unevenly down the sides.

PRUNE-BANANA COFFEE CAKE

This bread is a nutritious snack as well as a wonderful addition to breakfast.
9-inch round cake

1&1/2 cups flour
1 teaspoon salt
2 teaspoons baking powder
1/2 teaspoon baking soda
1/2 cup unprocessed bran (not cereal)
1/4 cup wheat germ
1/4 cup (1/2 stick) butter, room temperature
1 teaspoon vanilla
1/2 cup dark-brown sugar
1 egg
3 to 4 medium-size, very ripe bananas
1/2 cup pitted prunes, stewed and pureed

Topping:

1/4 cup *each* semi-sweet chocolate chips and walnuts, chopped
1/2 cup dark-brown sugar
1/2 teaspoon cinnamon
2 tablespoons (1/4 stick) butter, at room temperature

Preheat oven to 350°.

In small bowl, combine dry ingredients. Set aside.

In large bowl of electric mixer, beat butter. Add vanilla and sugar and beat until well blended. Add egg and beat again. Set aside.

In separate bowl, mash bananas. Add bananas and prunes to creamed batter and mix just to blend. On low speed, add dry ingredients, beating just until incorporated. Spoon into greased 9-inch springform pan. Set aside while making topping.

To make topping: Place all ingredients in work bowl of food processor or blender and process just until mixture is crumbly. Sprinkle evenly on top of batter in pan.

Bake for 1 hour or until toothpick inserted in center of cake comes out clean. Cool on wire rack for 15 minutes before removing sides of pan.

PRUNE-CRUMB COFFEE CAKE

A fruit-rich coffee cake that easily could become a specialty of the house.
9-inch square cake

2 cups buttermilk
  baking mix
3 tablespoons sugar
1/2 cup milk
1 egg
3 tablespoons frozen
  orange juice con-
  centrate, thawed
1 cup pitted prunes,
  chopped

Preheat oven to 400°.

In bowl, combine baking mix and sugar. In measuring cup, mix milk, egg, and orange juice concentrate; add to dry ingredients and stir to blend. Turn into greased 9-inch square pan. Smooth top. Sprinkle evenly with prunes, then cover with Crumb Topping. Bake for 20 to 25 minutes until toothpick inserted into center comes out clean and top is lightly browned.

Crumb Topping:
1/2 cup buttermilk
  baking mix
1/2 cup light-brown
  sugar
1 teaspoon nutmeg
2 tablespoons butter,
  softened
1/2 cup pecans,
  chopped

To make crumb topping: In small deep bowl, blend topping ingredients, except for nuts, with a fork or pastry blender. Stir in pecans.

YEAST BREADS

Bohemian Kolaches

Dough:

3 packages dry yeast

1 tablespoon sugar

1/2 cup warm water
(110° to 115°)

2 cups milk

1/2 cup sugar

1 teaspoon salt

1/2 cup (1 stick)
melted butter

3 egg yolks plus 1
whole egg, lightly
beaten

5 to 6 cups flour

Prune Filling:

2&2/3 cups pitted
prunes

1 cup prune liquid
(reserved from
cooking)

1/2 cup sugar

1 tablespoon lemon
juice

1 teaspoon grated
lemon peel

1/2 teaspoon *each*
cinnamon and
allspice

Melted butter

Although Iowa is located in the middle of America, it is a melting pot for many nationalities. Many of the cultures have survived through the years and traditional foods abound. Our friend Linda proudly shared with us her recipe for kolaches, which was given to her by her great-grandmother from Czechoslovakia.
3 to 4 dozen kolaches

To make dough: Combine yeast, 1 tablespoon sugar, and water in a small bowl. Let sit for 10 minutes.

Place milk in a small saucepan over medium-high heat. When bubbles form around edge, remove from heat. Cool to room temperature.

In large mixing bowl, combine 1/2 cup sugar, salt, and melted butter; add beaten eggs. Stir in 3 cups of the flour, mixing well. Thoroughly blend in yeast mixture and add enough flour to make a soft dough. Place dough in large, greased bowl, turning once to coat. Cover loosely with kitchen towel and let rise 1 hour or until doubled in size. While dough is rising, make prune filling.

To make prune filling: Combine prunes with enough water to cover in a medium-size saucepan. Bring to a boil and simmer 10 minutes. Drain, reserving enough liquid to make 1 cup. (You may need to add water.) Put prunes, prune

CONTINUED

liquid, and remaining ingredients in food processor or blender; process until smooth.

To assemble: Divide dough into three pieces. Roll each of these pieces into several dozen walnut-size balls. Place balls on greased cookie sheet and let rise 1 hour or until doubled in size. Make indentation in middle of each ball and fill with 1 tablespoon prune filling. Let rise 5 to 7 minutes.

Preheat oven to 400°.

Bake kolaches for 18 to 25 minutes or until golden brown. Brush lightly with melted butter. Allow to cool on wire racks.

CALIFORNIA BATTER BREAD

Use this fragrant, no-knead yeast loaf for wonderful toast and tasty cheese sandwiches.
1 loaf

Preheat oven 375°.

1 package dry yeast
1&1/4 cups warm
water (110° to 115°)
2 tablespoons (1/4
stick) butter, softened
2 tablespoons sugar
2 teaspoons salt
3 to 3&1/2 cups flour
1&1/2 cups pitted
prunes, diced
1 egg, beaten
1 tablespoon sesame
seeds

In large bowl, sprinkle yeast over water; stir to dissolve. Mix in butter, sugar, and salt. Add 2 cups of the flour. Beat with electric mixer or wooden spoon 2 minutes, scraping sides of bowl. Stir in enough of the remaining flour to make a soft dough. Cover and let rise in a warm place until doubled, about 45 minutes. Stir in prunes to blend evenly. Turn into a greased 9 x 5-inch loaf pan. Smooth top, poking prune pieces beneath surface. Cover and let rise in a warm place until batter reaches just above top of pan, about 45 minutes. Brush top with egg and sprinkle with sesame seeds. Bake for about 45 minutes until top is browned and loaf sounds hollow when tapped. Turn out of pan and cool on rack. Loaf may be wrapped and frozen.

FESTIVE FRUIT BREAD

This pretzel-shaped loaf adds festive flair to any holiday table.

1 large loaf

Dough:

1/2 cup milk

1/4 cup (1/2 stick) butter

3 tablespoons sugar

1&1/2 teaspoons vanilla

1/2 teaspoon salt

1 package dry yeast

1/2 teaspoon sugar

1/4 cup milk, warm to the touch

2 eggs, well beaten

3 to 3&1/2 cups flour

Filling:

2 tablespoons (1/4 stick) butter

1 large apple, peeled and thinly sliced

1 ripe pear, peeled and thinly sliced

2 tablespoons sugar

3/4 cup pear juice (available as baby food)

1&1/3 cups mixed dried fruit, cut into small pieces

1/4 cup peach schnapps

To make dough: In small saucepan over low heat, combine milk with 1/4 cup butter until butter melts. Add 3 tablespoons sugar, 1&1/2 teaspoons vanilla, and salt; stir to blend. Set aside.

In large bowl, stir yeast and 1/2 teaspoon sugar into warm milk. Cover and let stand 10 minutes.

Add milk mixture and eggs to yeast. Gradually stir in flour, 1 cup at a time, until slightly sticky dough forms. Turn dough out onto floured surface and knead until smooth and elastic, adding flour as necessary. This process usually takes 8 to 10 minutes.

Butter large bowl. Add dough and turn to coat entire surface. Cover bowl, set in warm place, and let dough rise until doubled in bulk, about 1&1/2 hours.

To make filling: While dough is rising, melt 2 tablespoons butter in heavy large skillet over medium heat. Add apple and pear slices and 2 tablespoons sugar; cook until fruit is tender, stirring occasionally. Add pear juice and dried fruit. Cover and simmer gently until fruit is soft, about 35 minutes. Add schnapps and stir over medium heat until mixture attains a jam-like consistency, about 5 minutes. Set aside.

For assembly:

1 tablespoon butter, room temperature

1&1/2 tablespoons sugar mixed with 1/2 teaspoon cinnamon

Milk

To assemble: After dough has doubled in bulk, punch down and knead an additional 4 minutes on a lightly floured surface. Cover dough and let rest for 10 minutes.

Roll dough into a 10 x 32-inch rectangle on lightly floured surface. Spread 1 tablespoon butter over dough, leaving a 1-inch unbuttered border. Sprinkle cinnamon sugar over butter and top evenly with fruit filling.

Starting at 1 long edge, roll dough into a tight cylinder in jelly-roll fashion. Using pastry brush, lightly moisten the seam and ends of the roll with milk. Pinch to seal.

Grease a cookie sheet with vegetable oil. Transfer the fruit roll to the cookie sheet, putting seam side down. Shape into pretzel form. Cover with towel and let rise until almost doubled, about 35 minutes.

Preheat oven to 350°.

When doubled, bake bread for 45 minutes or until richly browned. If bread browns too quickly, cover with aluminum foil, shiny side down. Cool on rack until lukewarm.

Icing:

1/2 cup powdered sugar

1&1/2 tablespoons milk

1/2 teaspoon vanilla

To make icing: Mix all ingredients until smooth. Drizzle over warm bread.

FRENCH FRUIT-NUT BREAD

This fruit bread is rich and dense. The fruits and nuts give it an exceptional taste and appearance. As with fruitcake, this bread improves with age and makes a delicious gift.
2 loaves

1/3 cup pitted prunes, cut into 1/2-inch pieces

1 cup dark raisins

1&1/2 cups dried pears, cut into 1/2-inch pieces

1/2 cup dried dates, cut into 1/2-inch pieces

2/3 cup boiling water

1/4 cup honey

1 teaspoon grated lemon peel

1/3 cup kirsch

1 package dry yeast

1/2 teaspoon sugar

1 cup warm water (110° to 115°)

1 egg, room temperature

2 teaspoons cinnamon

1 teaspoon ground anise seeds

3/4 teaspoon salt

In medium-size bowl, combine dried fruits. In small bowl, stir together hot water, honey, grated lemon peel, and kirsch; pour this mixture over fruits. Mix just until fruits are coated. Cover bowl of fruits with plastic wrap and let stand 6 hours or until fruits have absorbed most of liquid; stir occasionally.

In small bowl, dissolve yeast and sugar in 1/4 cup warm water. Let mixture stand 10 minutes, or until it foams. In medium-size bowl, combine yeast mixture with remaining 3/4 cup warm water, egg, cinnamon, anise, and salt. Mix until thoroughly blended. Gradually stir in 2&1/2 to 3 cups flour, enough to make a soft dough. On well-floured surface, knead the dough, adding as much of the remaining flour as needed until the dough is stiff and elastic. Form the dough into a ball and place in greased bowl; cover with plastic wrap and let rise 1 hour or until doubled in bulk.

3&1/2 to 4&1/2 cups
unbleached flour
1/2 cup *each* blanched
whole almonds and
hazelnuts
1/2 cup walnuts,
coarsely chopped
1 egg yolk
Reserved fruit liquid
Water

While dough is rising, drain fruit in a sieve; save syrup.

Preheat oven to 350°.

Combine almonds and hazelnuts on a cookie sheet. Toast in oven for 15 to 20 minutes, stirring occasionally. Coarsely chop hazelnuts and almonds. Combine with walnuts and set aside.

When dough has doubled in bulk, punch it down. On a well-floured surface, knead fruits and nuts into dough. (Fruits and nuts must be added gradually to be well incorporated into the dough.) Use as much of the remaining flour as necessary to prevent dough from sticking. Form dough into a cylinder about 4 inches in diameter. The dough will be lumpy because of the fruits and nuts.

Cut dough crosswise into 2 pieces of equal size. Pinch ends and fold under to that ends are smooth. With palms of hands, roll each piece to form a 15-inch long loaf. Place loaves 4 inches apart on a lightly greased baking sheet. Cover with towel and let rise about 1 to 1&1/2 hours or until doubled in bulk.

Preheat oven to 350°.

When bread has doubled in bulk, prepare egg wash by mixing egg yolk and reserved fruit syrup in small bowl. If glaze appears too thick, use water to thin to desired consistency. Brush

CONTINUED

tops and sides of loaves thoroughly with egg wash. Bake loaves for 15 minutes. Remove sheet from oven and brush loaves with additional egg wash. Bake another 30 to 35 minutes or until loaves are richly browned. Transfer loaves to wire rack to cool. When cool, top with glaze.

Vanilla Glaze:

1 teaspoon vanilla

2 tablespoons hot milk

2 cups powdered sugar

To make vanilla glaze: Combine glaze ingredients until smooth. Drizzle evenly over loaves. Allow glaze to dry before wrapping in plastic wrap. The breads should ripen 1 to 6 days at room temperature or they may be frozen for up to 3 months.

GRANDMOTHER'S SPICED PRUNE LOAF

*Old-fashioned loaf similar to raisin bread . . .
but better!*
2 loaves

2 packages dry yeast
1/3 cup warm water
  (110° to 115°)
2 teaspoons sugar
1/2 cup sugar
1/2 teaspoon *each*
  cinnamon and salt
1&3/4 cups scalded
  milk
1/4 cup (1/2 stick)
  melted butter
2 eggs, slightly beaten
6&1/2 to 7 cups flour
1/4 teaspoon nutmeg
Pinch of ground
  ginger
3/4 cup pitted prunes,
  chopped
2 tablespoons (1/4
  stick) butter,
  softened
3 tablespoons sugar
  mixed with 2
  teaspoons cinna-
  mon

Sprinkle yeast over water and add 2 teaspoons sugar. Cover and set aside 10 minutes.

In large mixing bowl, combine sugar, cinnamon, and salt. Stir in hot milk and allow to cool to lukewarm. Add yeast mixture, blending well. Mix in butter and eggs. Add 2&1/2 cups of the flour, nutmeg, and ginger. Mix well until flour is incorporated. Add prunes and enough of remaining flour to make soft dough. Beat well with wooden spoon. Turn dough out onto a lightly floured board and cover loosely with clean kitchen towel. Allow to rest 10 minutes. Knead dough until smooth, approximately 10 minutes. With sharp knife, cut dough into 2 equal parts. Cover and allow to rest 30 minutes.

On a lightly floured surface, roll out 1 piece of dough into a 9 x 8-inch rectangle. Spread with 1 tablespoon butter and sprinkle with half of cinnamon mixture. Starting at long edge, roll jelly-roll fashion to form a cylinder, pinching seam ends. Place in lightly greased 9 x 5-inch loaf pan. Repeat process with remaining dough. Cover and allow to rise until doubled.

Preheat oven to 400°.

CONTINUED

Bake breads in preheated oven for 10 minutes. Reduce heat to 375° and continue baking for 30 to 35 minutes. When bread is done, it should be golden brown and sound hollow when lightly tapped with fingers. Cool 5 minutes, then remove from pans. Cool on wire racks.

Vanilla Glaze:

1 teaspoon vanilla

1 to 2 tablespoons hot milk

2 cups powdered sugar

To make vanilla glaze: Mix ingredients together until smooth. Glaze should be the consistency of thick cream. If it is too thick, very slowly add more hot milk, 1 teaspoon at a time.

Place loaves on racks over waxed paper or aluminum foil. Pour glaze over loaves, allowing it to run down sides.

LOW-COUNTRY ROUND BREAD

A favorite of ours. These tall, round loaves are perfect for toasting and making sandwiches.
3 loaves

2 cups pitted prunes
1/2 cup warm water
 (110° to 115°)
1 teaspoon sugar
1/4 teaspoon ground
 ginger
2 packages dry yeast
1&1/2 cups warm
 water
1/2 cup sugar
2 cups flour
1/2 cup dried skim
 milk
1&1/2 teaspoons salt
3 eggs, well beaten
1/2 cup (1 stick)
 butter, room tem-
 perature
1 teaspoon cinnamon
2 tablespoons grated
 lemon peel
6 cups flour
Melted butter

Place prunes in medium-size saucepan with enough water to cover. Bring to a boil and simmer 10 minutes. Drain. In food processor or blender, puree prunes. Set aside.

In small mixing bowl, mix together 1/2 cup warm water, sugar, ginger, and yeast. Set aside for 10 minutes. Mixture should be foamy and bubbly.

In large mixing bowl, stir together 1&1/2 cups water, sugar, 2 cups flour, and dried milk. Add yeast mixture and stir well. Add salt, beaten eggs, butter, cinnamon, lemon peel, prunes, and 5 cups of the flour. Mix until dough pulls away from sides of bowl. Turn dough out on floured surface and knead thoroughly 5 to 8 minutes until smooth and elastic, adding more flour as necessary. Return dough to bowl and brush dough with melted butter to coat. Cover lightly and allow to rise until dough doubles in bulk.

Preheat oven to 350°.

Turn dough out onto board and knead it lightly several times. Then divide dough into 3 equal portions.

CONTINUED

Shape dough into balls and place in 3 greased 1-pound coffee cans; cans should be half full. Or form into loaves and place in 3 greased 9 x 5-inch loaf pans.

If baking dough in cans, brush dough with melted butter and allow to rise only to top of can before baking. Bake for 30 minutes. Remove bread from cans and cool on wire rack.

If making loaves, brush dough lightly with melted butter and allow to rise until doubled in bulk. Bake for 30 to 40 minutes. Remove bread from pans and cool on wire rack.

Oatmeal-Molasses Bread

This bread, a favorite among our families, is moist and sweet but nearly fat-free.
2 loaves

1 cup oatmeal
1 cup boiling water
1/2 cup molasses
2 teaspoons salt
1 tablespoon butter
3/4 cup pitted prunes
2 packages dry yeast
1/2 cup warm water
 (110° to 115°)
4&1/2 cups flour

Put oatmeal in large bowl and add 1 cup boiling water. Allow to stand 1 hour. Add molasses, salt, and butter, blending well.

Place prunes in small saucepan with enough water to cover. Bring to a boil and simmer 10 minutes. Drain. In food processor or blender, puree prunes. Set aside.

In small bowl, dissolve yeast in warm water and allow to stand 10 minutes. Add yeast and prunes to oatmeal mixture in large bowl, blending well. Add flour, 1 cup at a time, mixing well after each addition. Turn dough out onto lightly floured surface, kneading until smooth, about 10 minutes; add more flour as necessary. Grease a large bowl. Put dough in bowl and turn to coat all sides. Cover lightly and allow to rise 50 to 60 minutes.

When doubled in bulk, punch dough down and shape into loaves. Place in 2 greased 9 x 5-inch loaf pans. Cover and let rise 1 hour.

Preheat oven to 350°.

Bake for 45 to 50 minutes. Remove breads from pans and cool on racks.

DESSERTS

CAKES

Autumn Prune-Apple Cake

12 to 14 servings

Preheat oven to 325°.

2 cups sugar
1&1/2 cups oil
3 eggs
3 cups flour
2 teaspoons baking
soda
1 teaspoon *each* salt
and cinnamon
1/2 teaspoon ground
cloves
2 cups pitted prunes,
coarsely chopped
2 cups coarsely
shredded apples
1 cup walnuts,
chopped
Powdered sugar

In large bowl, beat sugar, oil, and eggs 2 minutes with electric mixer at medium speed. In another bowl, combine dry ingredients; gradually mix into egg mixture. Mix in prunes, apples, and walnuts at low speed to blend thoroughly. Spoon into greased and floured 10-inch tube pan; smooth top. Bake for 1&1/2 hours, until springy to the touch and toothpick inserted into center comes out clean. Cool in pan 15 minutes. Invert onto rack to cool completely. Place on serving plate and dust with powdered sugar.

Brandied Prune Torte

Serve this flourless cake at your next dinner party. It makes a beautiful presentation.
12 to 14 servings

Torte:

12 eggs, separated and
   at room tempera-
   ture
1/4 teaspoon salt
2 cups sugar
4&1/2 cups walnuts,
   finely ground

Preheat oven to 350°.

Butter 3 9-inch round cake pans. Line bottoms with waxed paper, butter the paper, and dust lightly with flour.

To make torte: In large bowl of electric mixer, beat egg whites and salt until stiff but not dry. In another bowl, beat egg yolks about 3 minutes or until thick and pale in color. Reduce speed and gradually add sugar. Increase speed to high and beat another 5 minutes. Fold half of the nuts into the yolks, then fold in one third of the whites and remaining nuts. Gently fold in remainder of egg whites. Divide batter among prepared pans. Bake for 45 to 50 minutes or until top springs back when lightly touched. During baking, cake will rise and sink. (Don't be alarmed if it is very thin.) When done, remove pans from oven, cut around sides of cake with sharp knife, then cover pans with rack and invert. When pans are cool to touch, lift them away from cake and remove paper.

**Cream-Cheese
   Filling:**

2 packages (8 ounces
   each) cream cheese,
   room temperature
1 cup powdered sugar
1/2 cup (1 stick)
   butter, room tem-
   perature
2 tablespoons vanilla

To make cream-cheese filling: In large mixing bowl, beat all ingredients until light and fluffy. Set aside.

Prune Topping:

2 cups pitted prunes

1/4 cup water

1/4 cup plus 2 table-
  spoons brandy

To make prune topping: In small saucepan, combine ingredients. Boil gently 7 to 10 minutes or until prunes are soft. Set aside to cool. In food processor or blender, puree prunes with any remaining liquid until prunes are nearly smooth.

To assemble: Place one layer of torte on serving platter and spread with one third of cream-cheese filling. Place second layer on top and spread with one third of cream-cheese filling. Place third layer on top and spread with remaining cream cheese. Carefully spread on prune topping, leaving 1/2-inch rim of cream cheese visible. If desired, decorate by reserving some of the cream-cheese filling and piping rosettes around the rim of the cake. Refrigerate and serve cold.

Note: To prevent cakes from sticking to wire racks, spray racks with no-stick cooking spray before using.

Grand Chocolate Prune Cake

Prunes and Armagnac come from the same region in France and are often used together in cooking. This cake takes some effort, but your labors will be rewarded with accolades because it is moist, rich, and sinfully delicious.
12 servings

2 cups pitted prunes

1/3 cup Armagnac or other brandy

3 tablespoons sugar

9 ounces semisweet chocolate, chopped

1/4 cup Armagnac

2 teaspoons instant coffee powder

3/4 cup plus

2 tablespoons (1&3/4 sticks) butter at room temperature, cut into 7 pieces

3/4 cup sugar

1 cup flour

1 teaspoon cinnamon

3/4 teaspoon allspice

5 eggs, separated and at room temperature

Pinch *each* of salt and cream of tartar

1/4 cup sugar

Combine prunes, 1/3 cup Armagnac, and 3 tablespoons sugar in saucepan. Bring to boil and simmer 15 minutes. Remove from heat and let sit for 2 hours. Puree entire mixture and set aside.

In large saucepan, melt chocolate with 1/4 cup Armagnac and coffee powder over low heat, stirring constantly. Whisk in butter, 1 piece at a time, until well incorporated with chocolate. Remove from heat. Stir in 3/4 cup sugar, flour, cinnamon, and allspice. Blend in egg yolks and allow mixture to cool slightly.

Preheat oven to 350°.

With electric mixer, beat egg whites, salt, and cream of tartar until soft peaks form. Slowly add 1/4 cup sugar and beat until almost stiff but not dry. Beat chocolate mixture and prunes to loosen and gently fold in one quarter of the whites. Fold this batter into remaining whites. Pour batter into greased and floured 10-inch round cake pan. Bake in center of oven for 45 to 50 minutes or until cake tester inserted in cake comes out clean. Cool in pan 25 minutes. Invert on rack and cool completely.

Raspberry Layer:

1/4 cup raspberry preserves

To make raspberry layer: Put raspberry preserves in small saucepan and heat to boiling. Strain preserves in sieve and discard seeds. Place cake on platter and spread remaining preserves on top. Set aside.

Chocolate Glaze:

6 ounces semisweet chocolate

6 tablespoons (3/4 stick) butter

1 tablespoon honey

1/4 teaspoon instant coffee powder

To make chocolate glaze: Stir all ingredients in top of double boiler over simmering water. When glaze is smooth, remove from heat and let sit for 10 minutes.

Place strips of waxed paper under cake to protect platter. Gradually spoon glaze over cake, allowing it to drip down sides. With metal spatula, spread glaze evenly around sides and top of cake. Refrigerate until 1 hour before serving. For a special treat, garnish with fresh raspberries.

MAIDA HEATTER'S
PRUNE AND WALNUT LAYER CAKE

This cake by dessert expert Maida Heatter consists of three layers enriched with buttermilk and sour cream. Mildly spiced, it is filled and covered with a mousse of chocolate and cream cheese. This is a complicated recipe, with a variety of sub-recipes, but the result is glorious.
24 portions

1/4 cup fine bread crumbs

Generous 1&1/2 cups stewed pitted prunes, tightly packed (see Notes)

3 cups minus 2 tablespoons sifted all-purpose flour

1 teaspoon baking soda

1/2 teaspoon double-acting baking powder

1/2 teaspoon salt

1 teaspoon cinnamon

1 teaspoon nutmeg

1 teaspoon cloves

2 tablespoons unsweetened cocoa powder (preferably Dutch-process)

Adjust two racks to divide the oven into thirds and preheat oven to 350°.

Butter three 9-inch round layer cake pans, line them with rounds of baking pan liner paper or waxed paper cut to fit, then butter the paper, dust all over with fine dry bread crumbs, and invert over paper and tap out excess crumbs. Set aside.

Coarsely chop the prunes (on a board with a large French chef's knife—or you can cut them with scissors) and place them in a wide strainer or colander over a bowl to drain, but not to dry completely (they add moisture to the cake).

Sift together the flour, baking soda, baking powder, salt, cinnamon, nutmeg, cloves, and cocoa and set aside.

In the large bowl of an electric mixer beat the butter until soft. Add the vanilla and 1&1/2

8 ounces (2 sticks)
unsalted butter
1 teaspoon vanilla
extract
1&3/4 cups granulated
sugar
3 eggs graded "large"
or "extra-large,"
separated
1/2 cup buttermilk
1/2 cup sour cream
8 ounces (generous 2
cups) walnuts, cut
or broken into
medium-size pieces
Chocolate–Cream
Cheese Mousse
Icing (recipe
follows)

cups of the sugar (reserve the remaining 1/4 cup of sugar) and beat to mix. Add the egg yolks and beat until incorporated. On low speed add the sifted dry ingredients in three additions, alternating with the buttermilk and then the sour cream, scraping the bowl with a rubber spatula and beating until smooth after each addition. Remove the bowl from the mixer and stir in the prunes and nuts. Set aside.

In the small bowl of electric mixer (with clean beaters) beat the egg whites until they hold a soft point. Reduce the speed slightly and gradually add the remaining 1/4 cup of sugar. Then beat again briefly at high speed only until the whites just barely hold a straight point when the beaters are raised.

In two additions fold the whites into the batter. Divide the batter among the pans and smooth the tops.

Bake for 35 to 40 minutes until the cakes just begin to come away from the sides of the pans, and until the tops spring back when they are pressed lightly with a fingertip in the middle. Do not overbake. Toward the end of the baking, if the cakes are not browning evenly, exchange the positions of the pans.

Let stand for 2 to 3 minutes and then cover each pan with a rack, turn the pan and rack over, remove the pan and paper lining, cover the cake with another rack, and turn it over again,

CONTINUED

leaving the cakes right side up to cool on racks.

Before icing the cake, prepare a wide, flat cake plate by placing four 12 x 4-inch strips of baking pan liner paper or waxed paper in a square pattern around the sides of the plate. Place one cake layer on the plate upside down (all three layers will be upside down). Check to see that it touches the papers all around. If you have a cake-decorating turntable, place the cake plate on it.

**Chocolate–Cream
Cheese Mousse
Icing:**

14 to 16 ounces
semisweet chocolate
(see Notes)

8 ounces cream
cheese, preferably at
room temperature

8 ounces (2 sticks)
unsalted butter

1 teaspoon vanilla
extract

1/2 cup plus 2
tablespoons
granulated sugar

2 eggs graded "large,"
separated

1 cup whipping cream

Pinch of salt

To make chocolate–cream cheese mousse icing: Break up the chocolate and place it in the top of a large double boiler over warm water on low heat. Cover with a folded paper towel (to absorb steam) and the pot cover and heat until almost completely melted. Then uncover and stir until completely melted. Remove the top of the double boiler and set aside briefly.

In the large bowl of an electric mixer beat the cream cheese and butter with the vanilla and 1/2 cup of the sugar (reserve the remaining 2 tablespoons of sugar) until well mixed. Add the melted chocolate (which should still be warm to help dissolve the granules of sugar) and beat well until the sugar is dissolved. Beat in the 2 egg yolks (reserve the whites), beating at high speed until the mixture is as smooth as honey and has lightened slightly in color. Set aside.

In a small bowl, with chilled beaters whip the cream until it is very firm or as firm as you can make it without taking any chance that it might turn to butter. (The safest way to do this is to use the mixer only until the cream holds a soft shape. Then finish the whipping with a whisk. That way you have better control of what is happening and there is less chance of overbeating.) Set aside.

In a clean small bowl, with clean beater beat the egg whites with the salt until the whites hold a soft shape. Reduce the speed to moderate and gradually add the remaining 2 tablespoons of sugar. Increase the speed again and continue to beat briefly only until the whites hold a straight shape when the beaters are raised, but not until they stiffen/dry. Set aside.

Without being too thorough, fold the whipped cream in two additions into the chocolate mixture, then add the beaten whites and continue to fold gently only until the mixtures are blended—do not handle any more than is necessary.

With a long, narrow metal spatula spread a layer of the icing a generous 1/2 inch thick over the bottom layer of cake. Place the second layer of cake upside down over the icing. Spread that with another generous 1/2 inch thick layer of icing. Cover with the top layer of cake (also upside down).

Spread a rather thick layer of the icing all around the sides, and then over the top. If you

CONTINUED

wish, reserve about 3/4 cup of the icing for decorating the cake. (To do this, place the icing in a small pastry bag fitted with #4 or medium-size star-shaped tube. Form a row of small rosettes just touching one another around the top rim of the cake.)

Decoration:

2 to 3 ounces milk chocolate

Unsweetened cocoa powder (preferably Dutch-process)

Confectioners' sugar

To add decoration: With a vegetable parer form small curls of milk chocolate, allowing them to fall onto a piece of waxed paper. With a large spoon or wide spatula gently transfer the curls to the top of the cake, placing them within the ring of rosettes, or, if you have not made rosettes, cover the top of the cake all the way to the edges. Make it a generous layer of chocolate curls.

Then sprinkle the top of the cake with unsweetened cocoa powder through a fine strainer, and cover with a layer of confectioners' sugar.

Caution: *Do not tilt the cake plate until the icing has been refrigerated or the layers will slide out of place. Hold the plate very carefully.*

Remove the strips of baking pan liner paper or waxed paper by pulling each one slowly toward a narrow end.

Refrigerate for at least several hours before serving. The cake should be very cold when it is served. Serve small portions.

Notes:
1. If you want to stew the prunes yourself, you will need a 12-ounce box of dried pitted prunes or 1 pound of prunes with pits. If you buy them already stewed, you will need a 1-pound 9-ounce jar.
2. Maida Heatter has made this with 14 ounces (27-ounce bars) of Poulain chocolate and also with 16 ounces (44-ounce bars) of Maillard's Eagle Sweet chocolate; she says it was wonderful both ways.

No-Carrots Carrot Cake

This cake is very rich, spicy, and moist. It is especially rewarding after raking leaves or taking a brisk walk on a chilly day.
1 2-layer cake

3&1/4 cups flour
2 teaspoons baking powder
1 teaspoon *each* baking soda, cinnamon, and cardamom
1/4 teaspoon ground ginger
1/2 teaspoon *each* ground cloves and nutmeg
1/2 teaspoon salt
1 tablespoon cocoa
1&1/2 cups pitted prunes
1 cup (2 sticks) butter, room temperature
2 cups light-brown sugar
4 eggs
1&1/4 cups buttermilk
1 teaspoon vanilla
1/2 cup walnuts, finely chopped

Preheat oven to 350°.

In medium-size bowl, sift together flour, baking powder, baking soda, spices, salt, and cocoa. Set aside.

In medium-size saucepan, place prunes and enough water to cover by 1/2 inch. Simmer prunes 10 minutes. Drain prunes, reserving 1/2 cup of cooking liquid. Puree prunes in food processor or blender. Set aside.

In large bowl of electric mixer, beat butter and sugar together until creamy. Add eggs, 1 at a time, beating well after each addition. Add dry ingredients alternately with buttermilk and reserved 1/2 cup of prune liquid to batter, beating well after each addition. Add vanilla. Fold prunes and walnuts into batter.

Spoon batter into 2 greased and floured 9-inch round cake pans. Bake for 35 to 40 minutes or until cake springs back when lightly touched in center. Let cool 10 minutes. Invert cakes onto wire racks. Frost when cooled.

**Cream-Cheese
  Frosting:**

1/2 cup (1 stick)
  butter, room tem-
  perature
1 package (8 ounces)
  cream cheese, room
  temperature
1 teaspoon vanilla
4 cups powdered
  sugar
1 cup walnuts, finely
  chopped (optional)

To make cream-cheese frosting: In small bowl of electric mixer, cream butter and cream cheese. Add vanilla. Gradually add powdered sugar and beat until fluffy. Spread a thin layer of frosting between layers and frost top and sides with remaining frosting. To decorate, press walnuts into sides of cake.

OLD-FASHIONED POUND CAKE

This cake is a family favorite with or without fruits and nuts.
8 to 10 servings

1&1/2 cups (3 sticks) butter, room temperature
3 cups sugar
6 eggs
3 cups flour
1 teaspoon baking powder
1 cup plus 2 tablespoons milk
2 teaspoons vanilla
1/3 cup *each* pitted prunes, dried apricots, and walnuts, chopped

In large mixing bowl, beat butter until fluffy. Add sugar and mix well. Add eggs, 1 at a time, mixing well after each addition. In small mixing bowl, stir flour and baking powder together. Add flour mixture and milk alternately to batter, beginning and ending with flour mixture. Add vanilla and beat 5 minutes at medium speed. Fold in prunes, apricots, and walnuts.

Pour batter into well-greased and floured 10-inch tube pan. Place in cold oven. Turn oven to 350° and bake approximately 1 hour and 10 minutes. Check cake frequently during last 10 minutes. The cake is done when top springs back when lightly touched. Remove from oven and turn cake out onto wire rack to cool.

PARTY GINGERBREAD

2 cups flour
2 tablespoons unprocessed bran (not cereal)
3/4 teaspoon salt
1 teaspoon baking soda
1/4 teaspoon baking powder
2 teaspoons ground ginger
1/2 teaspoon nutmeg
1 teaspoon cinnamon
1/4 teaspoon ground cloves
1/2 cup (1 stick) butter, room temperature
1&1/4 cups sugar
2 large eggs
1/3 cup strong black coffee
1 cup canned pumpkin
1/2 cup pitted stewed prunes, pureed
1/2 cup raisins

Topping:
1/3 cup dark-brown sugar
1/3 cup pecans, chopped
3/4 teaspoon cinnamon

This recipe was tested one snowy winter afternoon. Tired from a day's cooking, we boiled up a pot of tea, put our feet up, and indulged. We rated the bread as excellent and the mood warm and merry, hence the name of this bread.
8 servings

Preheat oven to 350°.

Sift together flour, bran, salt, baking soda, baking powder, and spices, and set aside.

In large bowl of electric mixer, cream butter. Add sugar and beat to mix. Add eggs and beat to mix. On low speed, gradually add half of the dry ingredients, scraping the sides of the bowl with a spatula. Stir in coffee. Add remaining dry ingredients and beat only until completely blended. Add pumpkin and prunes and beat until incorporated. Carefully fold raisins into mixture. Spoon into greased 9-inch springform pan and smooth the top. Set aside.

To make topping: Combine all ingredients. Sprinkle evenly over top of cake.

Bake for 1 hour and 10 minutes or until the top feels firm to the touch and a cake tester inserted in the middle comes out clean. Cool cake in pan for 10 to 15 minutes, then remove sides of pan and cool on rack.

SPICY BUTTERMILK CAKE

12 to 16 servings

1 cup pitted prunes

2 cups flour

1 teaspoon *each*
 baking soda, salt,
 cinnamon, nutmeg,
 and allspice

3 eggs

1&1/2 cups sugar

1 cup oil

1 cup buttermilk

1 teaspoon vanilla

1 cup walnuts or
 pecans, chopped

In small saucepan, place prunes with enough water to cover. Bring to a boil and simmer 10 minutes. Drain. In food processor or blender, puree prunes and set aside.

Sift flour, baking soda, salt, and spices together and set aside.

Preheat oven to 300°.

In large mixing bowl of electric mixer, beat eggs. Add sugar and oil and beat only to incorporate. Gradually add dry ingredients to batter and beat only until blended. Fold in buttermilk, prunes, vanilla, and nuts. Pour into a greased and floured 9 x 13-inch pan and bake for 1 hour or until top of cake springs back when touched with fingertip. While cake is still warm, pour icing over top.

Buttermilk Icing:

1 cup sugar

1/2 cup buttermilk

1/2 teaspoon baking
 soda

1/2 teaspoon vanilla

1 teaspoon white corn
 syrup

1/2 cup butter

To make buttermilk icing: In medium-size saucepan, mix all ingredients and bring to a boil. Boil 2 minutes. Remove pan from heat and stir until bubbles disappear. With fork tines, poke holes in top of warm cake and pour icing over top.

WALNUT-RUM CAKE

The recipe for the hard sauce that dresses this rum cake has been handed down through generations of an old New England family. Our boys don't need any excuse to eat it; they think it tastes as good on their fingers as it does on the cake!

1 loaf cake

2 cups flour
1/2 teaspoon salt
2 teaspoons baking powder
3/4 cup (1&1/2 sticks) butter, room temperature
1&1/2 cups sugar
4 eggs
5 tablespoons dark rum
3 tablespoons milk
1 cup prunes, pureed
1 cup walnuts, finely chopped

Hard Sauce:
1 egg white
1/3 cup butter, at room temperature
Dash of vanilla
Dash of nutmeg
Powdered sugar

Preheat oven to 325°.

In small mixing bowl, combine flour, salt, and baking powder. In large mixing bowl, beat butter and sugar until smooth. Add eggs, 1 at a time, beating well after each addition. Add dry ingredients to batter, beating until smooth. Blend in rum, milk, prunes, and walnuts. Mix thoroughly.

Pour batter into greased and floured 9 x 5-inch loaf pan and bake for 1 hour or until toothpick inserted in center comes out clean. Cool on wire rack 10 minutes. Remove cake from pan and place on wire rack until completely cool. Serve with dollop of hard sauce.

To make hard sauce: Beat egg white until it holds soft shape. Add butter and beat until creamy. Flavor with vanilla and nutmeg. Add powdered sugar until mixture reaches spreading consistency.

PIES
AND
PASTRIES

APRÈS-SKI TART

Hazelnut Crust:

1 cup hazelnuts (fil-
  berts), toasted
1/4 cup sugar
1 cup flour
1/4 teaspoon cinna-
  mon
1/8 teaspoon *each*
  nutmeg and allspice
1/8 teaspoon salt
7 tablespoons butter,
  cut into small
  pieces and at room
  temperature
1 egg yolk, room tem-
  perature

Fruit Filling:

3 cups prunes and
  other mixed dried
  fruit
3/4 cup dry white wine
2/3 cup honey
1/4 cup orange li-
  queur
1 teaspoon finely
  grated orange peel

Apricot preserves
1/4 cup hazelnuts,
  toasted and chopped

This hearty pie is best eaten by the fireside after a day of skiing or sledding. Accompany it with cups of hot mulled wine or steaming coffee.
8 to 10 servings

To make hazelnut crust: Finely chop the hazelnuts with sugar in a processor. Add flour, spices, and salt and process to blend. Add butter and egg yolk and mix until the dough begins to form a ball. Press the dough into greased 9-inch tart pan with removable bottom; make the sides at least 1/4 inch thick. Pierce bottom with fork several times. Refrigerate for 30 minutes or more.

Preheat oven to 350°.

Bake chilled crust until golden, 25 to 30 minutes. Cool on wire rack.

To make fruit filling: Combine dried fruits, wine, and honey in small, heavy saucepan. Cover and simmer until all liquid is absorbed, stirring occasionally, about 15 to 20 minutes. Cool 5 minutes. Stir in orange liqueur and orange peel.

Spread a thin layer of apricot preserves over bottom of baked crust. Pour filling into crust. Sprinkle fruit with chopped hazelnuts. Serve at room temperature. This pie can be prepared a day ahead.

CHEESE TART WITH PRUNES AND PORT

1 cup port

1&1/2 cups water

1-inch piece cinnamon stick

4 whole cloves

2 cups pitted prunes

Crust:

2/3 cup flour

3 tablespoons sugar

1/4 teaspoon cinnamon

1/4 cup (1/2 stick) cold butter, cut into small pieces

Filling:

3 packages (8 ounces each) cream cheese, softened

3 egg yolks

1 teaspoon vanilla

Peel from 1/2 lemon, finely grated

1 cup whipping cream

3 tablespoons sugar

3 egg whites, room temperature

1 tablespoon sugar

Prunes soaked in port add a new flavor to the classic cheesecake.
10 to 12 servings

In medium-size saucepan, combine first 5 ingredients and bring to a boil. Lower heat and allow to simmer 10 minutes. Remove from heat. Allow to cool.

Preheat oven to 350°.

To make crust: In food processor, process all crust ingredients until mixture just begins to form a ball. To make crust by conventional method, combine flour, sugar, and cinnamon in small bowl. Cut in butter with pastry blender or 2 knives until crumbly. Form into a ball. Press onto bottom of 9-inch springform pan. Bake for 10 minutes. Cool completely.

Preheat oven to 375°.

To make filling: In large bowl, combine cream cheese, egg yolks, vanilla, and lemon peel. Beat until light and fluffy. In separate bowl with clean beaters, beat whipping cream until soft peaks form. Gradually add 3 tablespoons sugar and beat until stiff. In another bowl with clean beaters, beat egg whites until soft peaks form. Add remaining 1 tablespoon sugar and beat until stiff. Carefully fold whipped cream and beaten egg whites into cream-cheese mixture.

To assemble: Drain prunes, discarding cinnamon stick and cloves. Place prunes on pie shell. Gently spread cream-cheese mixture over prunes. Bake for 50 to 55 minutes. Remove tart from oven and place on wire rack while making topping.

Preheat oven to 450°.

Sour-Cream Topping:

1&1/2 cups sour cream

2 tablespoons sugar

1 teaspoon vanilla

To make sour-cream topping: In small bowl, combine all ingredients. Spread evenly over cheesecake. Return tart to oven and bake for approximately 7 minutes, watching carefully to prevent sour cream from browning. Remove tart from oven and let cool at least 2 hours before serving or refrigerating.

CROUSTADE OF PRUNES

A crisp shell of paper-thin filo pastry encloses fruit in this elegant dessert.
6 to 8 servings

4 cups pitted prunes
1 teaspoon grated
  lemon peel
1&1/2 cups water
1/4 cup Armagnac *or*
  other brandy
1/4 cup sugar plus
  more for sprinkling
2 teaspoons vanilla
8 to 10 tablespoons
  (1 to 1&1/4 sticks)
  unsalted butter,
  melted
9 or 10 filo or strudel
  leaves, thawed (see
  Note)
Currant jelly
Powdered sugar

Soak prunes and lemon peel in water overnight. Drain and coarsely chop prunes; place in a bowl and pour Armagnac, sugar, and vanilla over them. Allow to stand at room temperature at least 1 hour.

Preheat oven to 400°.

Place a large cookie sheet on lowest oven rack. Lightly brush 15-inch pizza pan with some of melted butter.

Drain chopped prunes and reserve liquid.

Unroll thawed filo leaves. Place in stack in front of you and cover with slightly dampened towel. This prevents filo from drying out; replace towel each time you remove a piece. Working quickly, remove top leaf and lay flat on piece of waxed paper. Brush leaf lightly with melted butter; fold lengthwise in half; brush top side lightly with butter. Place buttered side down on pizza pan, putting one end of folded leaf at center of pan, extending other end over the side of pan. Brush lightly with melted butter and repeat with the remaining leaves, placing them spoke-fashion so that inner ends are stacked and outer ends just touch. Gently spread a thin layer of currant jelly over bottom of pastry in a 10-inch circle. Sprinkle parts of filo extending over edge of pan very lightly with some of the reserved liquid. Place fruit on top of jelly.

To enclose filling, start with the last filo leaf placed on pan. Lift end of this leaf and bring towards center of filling; twist the leaf one complete turn and lightly press down into filling. Repeat with remaining leaves in order, placing coils as closely together as possible to cover top of tart. (Do not be concerned if filling shows between strips.) Sprinkle top with reserved liquid; dust lightly with powdered sugar and drizzle with any remaining butter.

Place pizza pan in oven on hot cookie sheet. Bake for 12 minutes. Reduce oven temperature to 350°. Bake until tart is golden and crisp, another 20 to 25 minutes. Slide the tart from pizza pan onto a wire rack. Sprinkle with additional Armagnac and granulated sugar. Serve at room temperature. Prior to serving, dust with powdered sugar. Serving is made simpler by cutting tart with scissors.

Note: Filo or strudel leaves, usually frozen, are available in most large grocery or specialty markets.

FRENCH PRUNE TART

This delicious tart served on a rich custard sauce deserves gourmet status.
12 servings

4 cups pitted prunes

Place prunes in large bowl and add enough cold water to cover. Let stand overnight at room temperature.

Sauce:

1&3/4 cups half-and-half

4 egg yolks

Pinch salt

1/3 cup sugar

1 teaspoon vanilla

To make sauce: In medium saucepan, cook half-and-half over moderate heat until bubbles form around edge of pan. While it is cooking, place egg yolks in top of double boiler. When bubbles appear in the half-and-half, gradually add it to the yolks, stirring constantly. Mix in salt and sugar. Place top section over bottom of the double boiler. Cook cream mixture, stirring constantly until it coats wooden spoon. Remove top section of double boiler and stir in vanilla. Cool completely. Cover tightly and refrigerate until ready to serve. This sauce may be made a day ahead.

Pastry:

2 cups flour

1/2 cup sugar

7 tablespoons butter, chilled and cut into small pieces

2 eggs

To make pastry: Place flour and sugar in work bowl of food processor. Process 10 seconds. Add butter and process until mixture resembles coarse meal. Add eggs and process until dough forms a ball.

Gently pat dough into 10-inch tart pan with removable bottom, covering bottom and sides; make sides twice as thick as bottom. Refrigerate 1 hour.

Drain prunes thoroughly and pat dry with paper towel. Cut each prune in half and arrange attractively in pastry shell.

Preheat oven to 325°.

Filling:

3 eggs

3 tablespoons sugar

1 cup half-and-half

1 tablespoon kirsch

1 teaspoon vanilla

To make filling: In large bowl, beat remaining 3 eggs and sugar until well blended. Stir in half-and-half, kirsch, and vanilla. Pour mixture evenly over prunes. Bake until filling is set, approximately 1 hour or until knife inserted in center comes out clean. Cool tart to room temperature.

When ready to serve, spoon thin coating of sauce on dessert plate and top with slice of prune tart.

FRUITED PECAN TART

This tart makes breakfast or brunch a special occasion. Add a dollop of whipped cream with a pecan in the center to turn this tart into an elegant dessert.
6 to 8 servings

Preheat oven to 425°.

Pastry:
1 cup flour
1/4 teaspoon salt
2 tablespoons sugar
1/2 cup (1 stick) unsalted butter, chilled and cut into small pieces
1 egg yolk
1&1/2 tablespoons ice water

To make pastry: Combine flour, salt, and sugar in food processor with metal blade and process for a few seconds to blend. Add butter and egg yolk and process 5 to 10 seconds or until mixture resembles coarse cornmeal. With processor on, gradually add water until dough just begins to come together. You can make the crust without a processor as follows. In large bowl, combine flour, salt, and sugar. Cut in butter, using pastry blender, forks, or two knives, until mixture resembles coarse cornmeal. Add egg yolk and ice water. Stir with fork until dough forms into a ball.

Press dough into a 9-inch tart pan with removable bottom. Prick all over with a fork and chill for 15 minutes.

Bake tart shell for 12 to 15 minutes, watching carefully to make sure it doesn't get too brown. Remove tart shell from oven and set aside.

Apricot Glaze:

1/4 cup apricot pre-
   serves

To make apricot glaze: Place apricot preserves in a small saucepan and bring to a boil. Remove from heat. Strain preserves and discard pulp. Spread remaining preserves over bottom of cooled crust.

Reduce oven to 325°.

Filling:

1/2 cup pecans,
   chopped
1&1/4 cups pitted
   prunes
1/4 cup raisins
2 eggs
1 cup light-brown
   sugar
1 cup sour cream
1 teaspoon vanilla

To make filling: In food processor or blender, process pecans until finely chopped. Add prunes and raisins and process to puree the fruit. Add remaining ingredients and process until well blended. Pour mixture into prepared pie shell and bake for 30 minutes or until knife inserted in center comes out clean. Serve warm or cold.

Portuguese Prune Tart

Port adds a different flavor to this tart enriched with prunes. A small slice with a glass of port is an appropriate way to end an enjoyable evening.
10 to 12 servings

Prune Filling:

5 cups pitted prunes

1&1/3 cups sugar

1 cup water

1/4 cup port

2 tablespoons port

1 tablespoon vanilla

Pastry:

2 cups flour

2/3 cup sugar

1 tablespoon baking
 powder

1/4 teaspoon cinna-
 mon

Pinch of salt

3/4 cup (1&1/2 sticks)
 unsalted butter,
 well chilled and cut
 into small pieces

2 egg yolks

1 egg

Apricot preserves

1 egg, beaten lightly,
 for glaze

To make prune filling: Cook prunes, sugar, water, and 1/4 cup port in large saucepan over low heat until sugar dissolves. Increase heat and bring to a boil. Cover and simmer gently for 35 minutes, stirring frequently. Cool to room temperature. Puree prune mixture in food processor or blender, adding 2 tablespoons port and vanilla. This filling may be made the day before and stored at room temperature.

To make pastry: Mix flour, sugar, baking powder, cinnamon, and salt in a work bowl of food processor. Process 10 seconds. Add the butter. Process until mixture resembles coarse meal. Add egg yolks and egg and process until dough forms a ball. Divide dough into thirds, combining two thirds for bottom crust and keeping one third for lattice top. Wrap each piece in plastic wrap, flatten, and refrigerate at least 1 hour.

Grease and flour an 11-inch tart pan with removable bottom. Roll bottom crust between two layers of plastic wrap into 13-inch circle. Slide on cookie sheet and freeze 5 to 10 minutes. This makes the dough easier to work with and is a necessary step. Remove dough from freezer and peel back top sheet of plastic wrap carefully. Invert dough into prepared pan. Remove remaining plastic wrap and gently press dough into pan. If dough splits and breaks, pat into place. Refrigerate until firm, or overnight.

Spread a thin layer of apricot preserves over bottom of crust. Spoon prune mixture into the shell, spreading evenly with a spatula. Set aside. Roll remaining pastry disc between layers of plastic wrap into 12-inch square. Refrigerate or place into freezer until firm. Cut firm dough into long strips about 1/2 inch wide. Begin making lattice top by arranging half of strips horizontally across top of tart, spacing about 3/4 inch apart. Arrange remaining strips vertically in opposite direction, also 3/4 inch apart. Trim strips and press ends into the edges of shell, being careful not to extend over rim of pan. Refrigerate for at least 30 minutes.

Preheat oven to 375°.

Brush lattice with egg glaze. Bake tart until golden brown, about 45 minutes. If top browns too quickly, cover with aluminum foil for last 10 minutes of baking. Cool completely. Serve at room temperature.

WHIPS AND OTHER DESSERTS

APPLE-PRUNE DOWDY

There's nothing dowdy about this treat! It gets its name because you "dowdy" or break up the top to let the cream drizzle in.
6 to 8 servings

2 cups pitted prunes, halved

2 cups sliced apples

1 cup orange juice

1/4 cup light-brown sugar

1/2 teaspoon cinnamon

1/4 cup (1/2 stick) butter, softened

1/4 cup sugar

1 egg

3/4 cup flour

1 teaspoon *each* baking powder and grated orange peel

1/4 teaspoon salt

1/3 cup milk

Preheat oven to 350°.

In 1&1/2-quart shallow baking dish, layer prunes and apples; pour juice over and sprinkle with brown sugar and cinnamon. Cover and bake for about 30 minutes or until apples are tender.

Meanwhile, in mixing bowl, cream butter and sugar until fluffy. Beat in egg, flour, baking powder, orange peel, and salt. Stir in milk to blend thoroughly; spread evenly over fruit and continue to bake, uncovered, about 30 minutes until top is lightly browned. Break up the top before serving and top with cream or vanilla ice cream, if desired.

Armagnac-Prune Mousse

This mousse is elegant enough to serve at a formal dinner party and easy enough to become a family favorite.
6 to 8 servings

1&1/3 cups pitted prunes
1/4 cup water
7 tablespoons Armagnac
1 package unflavored gelatin
1/4 cup water
4 eggs, separated and at room temperature
2 egg whites, room temperature
10 tablespoons sugar
3/4 cup sour cream
Whipped cream (optional)
Chocolate shavings

Combine first 3 ingredients in nonmetallic bowl and let sit on counter overnight. The next day, puree and set aside.

Soften gelatin in another 1/4 cup water in a small heat-proof bowl. Set in pan of simmering water and stir until gelatin dissolves. Remove bowl from water.

In mixing bowl, beat 6 egg whites until foamy. Gradually add 4 tablespoons of the sugar and beat until whites are stiff but not dry. Set aside. In another mixing bowl, combine prunes, remaining 6 tablespoons of the sugar, and 4 egg yolks and blend well. Add gelatin and sour cream and beat well. Thoroughly fold whites into prune mixture. Pour into glass bowl and refrigerate until firm, approximately 5 hours.

Garnish with whipped cream and sprinkle liberally with chocolate shavings.

BASIC PRUNE WHIP

4 servings

In medium-size saucepan, combine prune puree and sugar. Cook over medium-low heat until thick. Remove from heat. Add lemon juice and salt and stir until well blended. Cool.

Preheat oven to 300°.

3/4 cup cooked pitted prunes, pureed
Sugar to taste
1 tablespoon lemon juice
1/8 teaspoon salt
3 egg whites, room temperature
Whipped cream (optional)

In medium-size mixing bowl, beat egg whites until stiff. Fold prune mixture carefully into egg whites. Spoon into 1&1/2-quart unbuttered baking dish. Place dish in larger shallow pan. Pour enough hot water into larger pan so that water level is half the depth of smaller dish. Bake for 45 minutes or until firm when pressed lightly with finger. Serve at room temperature. Top with whipped cream, if desired.

CHILLED PRUNE WHIP

This dish doesn't require oven baking and so is a perfect finale to dinner on a warm summer's day. If you omit the walnuts, it's also a low-cholesterol dessert.
6 to 8 servings

1&1/2 cups pitted prunes

1&1/2 cups water

2 tablespoons lemon juice

3 egg whites, room temperature

1/4 teaspoon salt

1/3 cup sugar

1/4 cup walnuts, chopped

Combine prunes and water in small saucepan and bring to a boil. Cover and simmer for 10 minutes. Remove pan from heat and let cool. Drain cooled prunes; cut into small pieces; stir in lemon juice and set aside.

In medium-size mixing bowl, beat egg whites with salt until soft peaks form. Gradually add sugar, beating whites until stiff but not dry. Fold egg whites and walnuts together. Gently fold prune and lemon mixture into egg whites and walnuts. Put into individual serving bowls. Chill before serving.

OLD-FASHIONED RICE PUDDING

Handed down through the generations, this pudding recipe was always a favorite at Grandma Whitaker's Sunday suppers.
4 to 6 servings

Preheat oven to 300°.

4 cups milk
3/4 cup sugar
Pinch salt
2 tablespoons (1/4 stick) butter
3 tablespoons long-grain white rice, uncooked
1/3 cup pitted prunes, chopped
1/2 teaspoon vanilla
Nutmeg

In 5- to 6-cup ovenproof bowl, mix milk, sugar, salt, butter, and rice. Bake uncovered for 2 hours. Stir several times during that time. Remove from oven and add prunes and vanilla. Stir well and sprinkle with nutmeg. Bake 1 hour longer. Serve warm or chilled.

PRUNE AND ARMAGNAC ICE CREAM

This rich ice cream laced with Armagnac requires planning ahead. It is a gracious addition to a summer luncheon.
8 servings

2 cups pitted prunes
Armagnac or other
  brandy
3 cups milk
1 cup whipping cream
1 vanilla bean
8 egg yolks
1 cup sugar

In nonmetallic container, cover prunes with Armagnac. Seal tightly with plastic wrap. Set aside in a cool place for 2 to 6 weeks.

When ready to make ice cream, combine milk and cream in medium saucepan. Split vanilla bean in half lengthwise, scrape out seeds, and add both seeds and pod to cream mixture. Bring mixture to a simmer over medium heat. Cover, remove from heat, and let steep for 10 minutes.

In large bowl, whisk egg yolks and sugar together until lemon colored and thick. Gently whisk warm cream mixture into yolks. Return mixture to saucepan and cook over low heat, stirring constantly, until custard coats the back of a wooden spoon. Do not let custard boil or it will curdle. Remove and discard vanilla pod. Let custard cool completely.

Strain prunes and puree them in food processor. Stir puree into custard and chill thoroughly. Transfer to ice-cream maker and freeze according to manufacturer's instructions.
Note: When straining prunes, you can reserve the Armagnac to serve as an after-dinner drink with ice cream.

SPIRITED PRUNE BREAD PUDDING

Rum-soaked prunes make this old-fashioned dessert something special.
8 to 10 servings

1&1/2 cups pitted prunes, halved
1/3 cup rum
12 (1/2-inch thick) slices stale French bread (about 8 ounces)
6 eggs
1/2 cup sugar
1/4 cup light-brown sugar
1 cup whipping cream
3 cups milk
2 teaspoons grated orange peel
Powdered sugar

In bowl, combine prunes and rum; set aside 1 to 2 hours.

Preheat oven to 400°.

Line bottom of shallow 2- to 3-quart baking dish with half the bread. Spoon prune mixture over bread. Cover with remaining bread, overlapping slices slightly.

In large bowl, whisk together eggs, sugars, and cream. Stir in milk and orange peel. Pour over bread in baking dish. Press down lightly to thoroughly saturate bread. Bake in lower half of oven for 40 to 50 minutes, just until set. Cool 15 minutes. Lightly dust top with powdered sugar. Glaze for a few seconds under broiler. Serve warm or chilled.

DESSERTS

COOKIES

CHEWY CHOCOLATE NUGGETS

Flavorful chocolate drop cookies with mellow prunes and crunchy nuts—fast to make and fast to disappear.
About 4 dozen cookies

Preheat oven to 375°.

1/2 cup (1 stick) butter, room temperature
1 cup light-brown sugar
1/2 cup milk
1 teaspoon baking soda
1 egg
1&1/2 cups flour
1/3 cup cocoa powder
1&1/2 cups prunes, coarsely chopped
1/2 cup nuts, chopped
1/2 cup semisweet chocolate chips
Powdered sugar (optional)

In large bowl, cream butter and brown sugar. Mix milk with baking soda; add to butter mixture with egg. Beat to blend together. (Mixture will appear curdled.) Mix in flour and cocoa to blend thoroughly. Stir in prunes, nuts, and chocolate chips. Drop by heaping teaspoonfuls, spaced 2 inches apart, onto greased baking sheets. Bake for 8 to 10 minutes, just until springy to touch. Remove to racks to cool. Dust with powdered sugar, if desired.

CHOCOLATE FRUIT BALLS

No baking needed for these candylike cookies.
50 cookies

1 cup walnuts
1&1/2 cups raisins
2/3 cup pitted prunes
Grated peel of 1 orange
2 teaspoons almond
  extract
2 to 3 tablespoons
  brandy
1 pound semisweet or
  bittersweet chocolate
  (do not use chips)

In work bowl of food processor with metal blade in place, finely process a few walnuts at a time. Be careful not to grind nuts too finely because walnuts tend to get oily. Remove nuts and set aside. In same work bowl, grind raisins and prunes. Add to walnuts. Add remaining ingredients, except chocolate, and mix well. Form into small balls about the size of a walnut and let stand overnight, lightly covered with plastic wrap.

In top of double boiler, melt chocolate over simmering water. Pierce fruit balls with a toothpick and dip them in chocolate until they are fully coated; allow excess chocolate to drip off. Place balls on cookie sheets lined with wax paper. Refrigerate until chocolate is firm. Remove balls with spatula and store in airtight containers.

EARLY RISER PRUNE COOKIES

Healthy grains boost the nutrition in this breakfast cookie for those on the go. Make a double batch and freeze extras for long-term storage.
12 large cookies

3/4 cup (1&1/2 sticks) butter, room temperature

1/2 cup light-brown sugar

1 egg

1 teaspoon vanilla

2 cups rolled oats

3/4 cup whole-wheat flour

1/3 cup unprocessed bran (not cereal)

1&1/2 teaspoons allspice

1/2 teaspoon baking soda

1/4 teaspoon salt

1 cup *each* pitted prunes and walnuts, chopped

1 cup shredded apple (1 medium-size apple)

Preheat oven to 350°.

In bowl of electric mixer, cream butter, sugar, egg, and vanilla. Combine oats, flour, bran, allspice, baking soda, and salt; blend into creamed mixture. Stir in prunes, walnuts, and apple. Drop by generous spoonfuls onto lightly greased baking sheets. Flatten to 1/2 inch thick. Bake for 15 minutes or until lightly browned. Cool on racks. Store in airtight container. You can freeze securely wrapped cookies.

ENERGY BARS

This bar cookie was an instant success with all of our families. Tucked in a backpack or bag lunch, these bars are guaranteed to add zip to your day.
2&1/2 dozen bars

1 cup (2 sticks) butter, room temperature

1 cup light-brown sugar

1 cup *each* quick-cooking oats, flour, and whole-wheat flour

1/2 cup wheat germ

4 eggs, well beaten

1 cup *each* whole almonds and semisweet chocolate chips

1/2 cup *each* pecans, dried apricots, and pitted prunes, chopped

1/2 cup shredded coconut

1/2 cup light-brown sugar

Preheat oven to 350°.

In large mixing bowl, cream butter and 1 cup sugar until light and fluffy. Add oats, flours, and wheat germ and mix well. Press dough evenly into lightly greased 9 x 13-inch pan.

Combine remaining ingredients and mix thoroughly. Pour batter over dough and spread evenly. Bake for 35 minutes or until well browned. Cool to room temperature. Cut into bars and store in airtight container.

FRUITY SNACK BARS

This easy recipe produces spicy bars. They travel well and make a tasty addition to your picnic basket.
30 bars

2&1/4 cups flour

2 tablespoons unprocessed bran (not cereal)

1 teaspoon *each* baking powder and cinnamon

1/2 teaspoon *each* baking soda and salt

1/4 teaspoon allspice

1/8 teaspoon ground cloves

1/2 cup raisins

1/3 cup *each* pitted prunes, dried apricots, and dried peaches, chopped

3/4 cup walnuts, chopped

1/2 cup (1 stick) butter, room temperature

1 cup light-brown sugar

1 egg

1/4 cup orange juice

1 teaspoon vanilla

Preheat oven to 375°.

In medium bowl, combine dry ingredients. Add fruits and nuts and stir until well coated. Set aside.

In large mixing bowl, cream butter and sugar. Add egg, orange juice, and vanilla, blending well. Fold in dry ingredients. Spread batter evenly into 9 x 13-inch greased baking pan. Bake for 20 minutes or until knife inserted in center comes out clean. Cool on wire rack. Cut into squares.

LEMON-PRUNE BARS

These cookies are nice to have around when friends drop by on a lazy summer afternoon. Serve these bars with tall, cold glasses of lemonade.
2&1/2 dozen bars

Filling:

2 cups pitted prunes

1/4 cup raisins

1 teaspoon finely grated lemon peel

1 can (6 ounces) frozen lemonade concentrate

3/4 cup water

2/3 cup sugar

1/4 cup flour

Crust:

1 cup light-brown sugar

1&3/4 cups flour

1/2 teaspoon baking soda

1 teaspoon salt

3/4 cup (1&1/2 sticks) butter, cut into 6 to 8 pieces

1&1/2 cups rolled oats

1/2 cup walnuts, chopped

To make filling: In food processor or blender, puree prunes and raisins. Transfer to medium-size saucepan and add lemon peel, lemonade, and water. Cover and simmer 15 to 18 minutes. Blend in remaining ingredients. Set aside to cool.

Preheat oven to 400°.

To make crust: In food processor fitted with metal blade, process sugar, flour, baking soda, and salt to blend. Add butter and process with on-off pulses until mixture resembles coarse cornmeal. Add oats and walnuts; process to blend. To make crust by hand, combine dry ingredients in large bowl. Cut in butter using pastry blender or two knives until mixture is crumbly.

Press half of mixture into bottom of greased 9 x 13-inch pan. Spread with cooled prune filling, leaving 1-inch border on all sides. Crumble remaining crust over top of filling. Bake for 25 to 30 minutes or until light brown. Cut into bars when cool.

NEWTONS OF IOWA CITY

In 1895, Kennedy Biscuit Works, in Cambridge-port, Massachusetts, acquired a machine that made dough into an enclosed wrap-around sandwich firm enough to hold a filling. They created a stuffed cookie using their most successful jam—fig. When it was time to name the cookie, it was agreed that "fig" and the name of a nearby town should be used. "Fig Boston" just didn't sound right! An employee from Newton, Massachusetts, suggested Newton and history speaks for itself. Not to be outdone by the Fig Newton, we developed a newton of Iowa City that is a big hit with our children.

40 bars

Pastry:

6 tablespoons (3/4 stick) butter, room temperature

1/3 cup light-brown sugar

2 eggs

1 teaspoon vanilla

2 cups flour

2 tablespoons unprocessed bran (not cereal)

1/2 teaspoon salt

1/4 teaspoon baking soda

Filling:

1 cup *each* pitted prunes and dried apricots

1/4 teaspoon grated lemon peel

2 cups water

1/3 cup sugar

1 teaspoon lemon juice

To make pastry: In food processor fitted with metal blade, process butter, sugar, eggs, and vanilla until blended. Add dry ingredients and process using on-off pulses until dough forms a ball. To make pastry using mixer, combine all ingredients in bowl of electric mixer and beat until well combined. Form into a ball. Wrap in plastic wrap, flatten slightly, and refrigerate for 2 to 3 hours.

To make filling: In medium saucepan, combine prunes, apricots, lemon peel, and water. Bring to a boil, lower heat, and simmer uncovered 20 minutes or until most of the water is absorbed. In food processor or blender, process fruit using 3 on-off pulses. Return fruit to saucepan and add sugar. Cook slowly, stirring constantly,

CONTINUED

until fruit thickens. Stir in lemon juice and allow mixture to cool.

Preheat oven to 350°.

Divide dough in half. Return 1 half of dough to refrigerator. Roll remaining dough between 2 pieces of waxed paper until it measures 10 x 10 inches. Remove waxed paper. Using a sharp knife, trim edges to form a neat square. Cut dough into 2 rectangles. Spread 1/2 cup filling down center of first rectangle. Bring sides of dough together over filling, forming a cylinder. Pinch seam lightly. Repeat procedure with other rectangle.

Place both rolls, seam side down, on greased baking sheet, at least 3 inches apart. Bake for 20 minutes or until firm and golden brown. Allow to cool on baking sheet at least 5 minutes before removing to wire rack to cool completely.

Make 2 more rolls, using remaining refrigerated dough and filling, and bake as directed.

Cut into 1-inch slices and store at room temperature or refrigerate.

PLUMP PRUNE PILLOWS

*Each little pastry is stuffed with a juicy surprise
. . . especially good with a cup of coffee or a
glass of milk.*
20 cookies

20 pitted prunes

1/4 cup brandy *or*
water

1 cup flour

1/4 cup sugar

1/2 cup (1 stick)
butter, room tem-
perature

1 package (3 ounces)
cream cheese, soft-
ened

1 egg, beaten

1/4 cup nuts, finely
chopped

In small bowl, combine prunes and brandy; cover and set aside at least 3 hours, stirring occasionally. In bowl, combine flour and 2 tablespoons of the sugar. Cut butter and cream cheese into 1-inch chunks; add to flour mixture. Work with pastry blender until mixture resembles coarse cornmeal. Gather into a ball, flatten slightly, and wrap in waxed paper. Chill 1 hour.

Preheat oven to 375°.

Drain prunes. On lightly floured board, roll out pastry in 1/8-inch thick rectangle. Cut into 20 pieces about 3 inches square. For each "pillow," place a drained prune in center of pastry square. Brush edges with egg. Bring up opposite corners and seal to enclose prune. Place on baking sheet, spaced 1 inch apart. Brush with egg. Sprinkle with nuts, then with the remaining sugar. Bake for 20 to 25 minutes until lightly browned. Remove to racks to cool. Store in airtight container.

PRUNE CHOCOLATE-CHIP COOKIES

In 1930, Ruth Wakefield, owner of The Toll House Inn, was making cookies when she ran out of cocoa. She used chocolate bits instead, assuming they would melt. The bits kept their shape and the cookies were a hit with her guests. In 1989, Donna created her own special chocolate chip cookie that added the all-important ingredient . . . prunes!
3 dozen large cookies

1 cup (2 sticks) butter, room temperature
1/2 cup sugar
1 cup dark-brown sugar
1 egg
2&1/4 cups flour
2 teaspoons baking powder
3/4 teaspoon baking soda
1 teaspoon salt
1 cup quick-cooking rolled oats
1/4 cup wheat germ
2 tablespoons unprocessed bran (not cereal)
1 cup macadamia nuts
1 cup milk chocolate chips
1 cup pitted prunes, cut into raisin-size pieces

Preheat oven to 350°.

In large bowl of electric mixer, cream butter and sugars. Beat in egg. On low speed, gradually add flour, baking powder, baking soda, and salt. Add remaining ingredients and beat only until blended. Drop dough by tablespoonfuls onto greased cookie sheets, 3 inches apart. Bake for 15 to 18 minutes. Cool cookies on rack.

PRUNE GEMS

3&1/2 dozen cookies

With food processor, process first 4 ingredients until blended. Add dry ingredients, processing until mixture forms a ball. Wrap in plastic wrap, flatten slightly, and chill for 2 to 3 hours.

1/2 cup (1 stick) butter

1 cup sugar

2 eggs

1 teaspoon vanilla

2&1/2 cups flour

1/4 teaspoon baking soda

1/2 teaspoon salt

1 can (12 ounces) Solo or Baker prune filling

Preheat oven to 400°.

On floured surface, roll dough to 1/16 inch thick and cut with 2&1/2-inch round cookie cutter. Place half of circles on greased cookie sheet, 1 inch apart. Spread 1 teaspoonful of prune filling over circle, leaving a narrow edge uncovered. Place remaining circles over cookies on baking sheet. Press edges together with floured fork. Bake for 8 to 10 minutes or until cookies are light brown. Dust with powdered sugar while still warm.

PRUNE HAMANTASCHEN

These triangular cookies are a traditional treat served during Purim, the "Feast of Lots." This festive Jewish holiday commemorates the time when Haman, second in command to King Ahasuerus, schemed to exterminate the Jews living in Persia in the fifth century B.C. Lots were drawn to determine the day of the massacre. Queen Esther's cousin, Mordecai, warned her of the impending danger. Queen Esther begged the King to nullify the decree and the Jews were spared. Hamantaschen is eaten to remind Jews of the three-cornered hat Haman wore.

45 cookies

5&1/2 cups flour

3 tablespoons baking powder

1&1/2 teaspoons salt

4 eggs

1 cup oil

1 tablespoon vanilla

1&1/4 cups sugar

1 to 2 cans (12 ounces each) Baker or Solo prune filling

Preheat oven to 350°.

In small bowl, combine first 3 ingredients and set aside.

In large mixing bowl, combine eggs, oil, vanilla, and sugar with wooden spoon. Gradually add flour mix, adding only enough to make the dough pliable and easy to roll out. On floured surface, roll out dough to 1/4-inch thickness. Cut with 3-inch round cookie cutter. Place about a tablespoon of filling in center of dough. Fold sides of dough to meet over filling, pinching to make a triangular cookie. Transfer cookies to greased cookie sheets and bake for 30 to 40 minutes or until cookies are light brown. Cool on wire racks.

PRUNE MACAROONS

Children love these sweet and crunchy cookies.
3 to 4 dozen cookies

Preheat oven to 350°.

3/4 cup pitted prunes, cut into raisin-size pieces
1/4 cup raisins
1/2 cup plus 2 tablespoons sweetened condensed milk
1/4 teaspoon salt
1/2 teaspoon vanilla
1 cup shredded coconut
2 cups Total or Special K cereal
Candied cherries

In large mixing bowl, combine all ingredients, except cherries, with a wooden spoon until well blended. With fingers, shape dough into walnut-size balls. Place on greased cookie sheets. Top each cookie with a candied cherry. Bake for 10 minutes.

PRUNE SQUARES

These fruity squares encased in a rich, yeast dough make a nice addition to brunch.
15 squares

1&1/2 cups cooked prunes, drained and pureed
1/2 cup sugar
1/4 cup finely chopped pecans *or* walnuts
1/4 cup milk
1 package dry yeast
1/4 cup warm water (110° to 115°)
1/2 teaspoon salt
2&1/4 cups flour
1/4 cup (1/2 stick) butter
1 egg

In small glass bowl, combine prunes, 1/4 cup of the sugar, and nuts. Reserve.

In small saucepan, scald the milk. Set aside to cool.

In small bowl, sprinkle yeast on warm water and stir to dissolve. Let sit 10 minutes.

In work bowl of food processor, combine remaining 1/4 cup of the sugar, salt, and flour; process 10 seconds. Add butter and process until mixture resembles coarse cornmeal. Add milk, yeast, and egg; process until dough begins to pull away from sides of bowl and forms into a ball. Place dough in large greased bowl, turning dough once. Cover, place in warm spot, and let dough rise 1 to 1&1/2 hours or until doubled in size. When doubled, turn dough onto floured board and divide in half. Cover; let rest another 10 minutes.

Roll out each half of dough to make a 12 x 16-inch rectangle. Carefully place 1 rectangle on greased baking sheet. Spread with prune mixture. Leave about a 1/2-inch border on all 4 sides. Place other rectangle on top and crimp edges. Let rise 1 hour.

Preheat oven to 350°.

Bake for 30 minutes or until light brown. Cool 10 minutes and then top with Orange Frosting. Cut into squares to serve.

Orange Frosting:

1 cup powdered sugar

1/4 teaspoon grated orange peel

1 tablespoon orange juice

To make orange frosting: In small bowl of electric mixer, beat frosting ingredients together. Add more orange juice, if needed, until frosting is the right consistency for spreading.

SOFT GRANOLA BARS

These soft, chewy bars are more nutritious than commercial granola bars and are a huge success with children.
40 bars

1 cup dark-brown
   sugar
1 cup oil
2 eggs
2 cups rolled oats
3/4 cup *each* flour and
   whole-wheat flour
1/3 cup *each* pitted
   prunes and dates,
   chopped
1/3 cup raisins
1 cup walnuts or
   pecans, chopped
2 teaspoons cinnamon
1 teaspoons *each*
   ground clove and
   baking soda
1/4 teaspoon salt
1/2 cup semisweet
   chocolate chips

Honey Glaze:
2 tablespoons butter
1/4 cup honey

Preheat oven to 350°.

In large bowl, mix sugar, oil, and eggs. Beat until smooth. Stir in remaining ingredients. Spread evenly in greased 10 x 15-inch jelly-roll pan. Bake for 17 to 22 minutes or until center is just set but not firm. Cool 15 minutes.

To make honey glaze: Melt butter in small saucepan over low heat. Stir in honey and mix until glaze is heated through. Drizzle glaze evenly over bars. Cool completely before cutting. Can be stored in airtight container for 2 weeks or frozen for up to 6 months.

SPICED PRUNE DROPS

These easy cookies are soft, chewy, and full of spices.
4 dozen drops

1&3/4 cups flour
1/2 teaspoon *each* baking soda, salt, and ground cloves
1 teaspoon *each* nutmeg and cinnamon
1/8 teaspoon allspice
1/2 cup (1 stick) butter, room temperature
1 cup light-brown sugar
1 egg
1/4 cup milk
1 cup pitted prunes, cut into raisin-size pieces

Preheat oven to 400°.

In small bowl, combine dry ingredients. Set aside.

In large mixing bowl, beat butter, sugar, and egg until fluffy. Add dry ingredients alternately with milk, beginning and ending with dry ingredients. Fold in prunes. Drop dough by teaspoonfuls onto greased cookie sheets. Bake for 8 to 10 minutes. Cool on wire racks.

Symphony Squares

These cookies take some time to make but are worth the effort.
40 to 50 bars

Preheat oven to 350°.

Dough:
2 packages dry yeast
1/4 cup warm water
  (110° to 115°)
1&1/2 cups (3 sticks)
  butter, room
  temperature
4 cups flour
4 egg yolks, lightly
  beaten
1/4 cup milk

Nut Filling:
2 cups (1 pound) wal-
  nuts or pecans,
  finely ground
1 cup sugar
1 teaspoon cinnamon

1 can (12 ounces)
  Solo prune filling

To make dough: In 2-cup measuring bowl, mix together yeast and water. Let stand about 10 minutes.

In large mixing bowl, combine butter and flour with a wooden spoon. Add egg yolks and milk. Mix well. Stir in yeast mixture. On a floured board, knead dough until it is no longer sticky, adding more flour if necessary.

To make nut filling: In small bowl, combine nuts, sugar, and cinnamon.

Divide dough into 3 balls. Roll out the first ball into the size of a large cookie sheet, 10 x 15 inches. Carefully transfer dough to cookie sheet. Spread half of nut mixture over sheet of dough. Leave a 1/2-inch border on all 4 sides. Roll out second ball of dough to the same size as first one and place it on top of nut mixture. Spread a layer of prune filling over dough. Again, leave a 1/2-inch border on all sides. Roll out the last ball of dough and place it over the prune filling. Crimp the edges together as you would for a pie crust. It is important that the edges be sealed. Bake for 25 to 30 minutes or until pastry is light brown. Cool.

Frosting:

3&3/4 cups (1 pound box) powdered sugar

3 tablespoons butter, room temperature

Orange juice or milk

To make frosting: In large mixing bowl, beat powdered sugar and butter together. Add enough orange juice to bring frosting to spreading consistency. Spread over top of pastry and sprinkle with remaining nut mixture. Cut into bars.

Note: These cookies may be frozen after baking.

BEVERAGES

GOOD MORNING BRACER

Packed with nutrition, this is sure to put a sparkle in your eye.
1 10-ounce drink

1/4 cup prune juice
1/4 cup unflavored
low-fat yogurt
4 pitted prunes
1 egg
1 tablespoon *each*
frozen orange juice
and cranberry juice
concentrate
1 tablespoon unproc-
essed bran (not
cereal)
4 ice cubes
2 tablespoons chilled
sparkling water

Combine prune juice, yogurt, prunes, egg, juice concentrates, and bran in electric blender. Blend smooth. Add ice; blend smooth. Pour into tall glass; stir in sparkling water.

PJ Magic

There's nothing like a little magic stashed away in the refrigerator! You can easily transform this mixture into a variety of inviting drinks.
2 quarts

3 cups prune juice
2&1/2 cups *each* apple
  juice and cranberry
  juice
1/2 *each* orange and
  lemon, thinly sliced

Combine all ingredients. Cover and store in refrigerator up to 1 week. Drink as is or enjoy in the following variations.

Meal in a glass: In electric blender, combine 1 cup PJ Magic, 1/2 cup unflavored yogurt, 1 egg, and 4 or 5 ice cubes. Blend until smooth. Makes about 2 cups.

Thick shake: In electric blender, combine 1 cup PJ Magic and 1 cup vanilla ice cream. Blend until smooth. Serve with straw and spoon. Makes 2 cups.

Ice-cream soda: Scoop 1/2 to 3/4 cup vanilla ice cream into tall glass. Add 3/4 cup PJ Magic. Splash with sparkling water, stir. Serve with straw and spoon. Makes 1 drink.

Spritzer: Pour 1 cup PJ Magic over ice cubes in tall glass. Splash with sparkling water. Garnish with lemon wedge and mint sprig, if you wish. Makes 1 drink.

Hot bracer: In small saucepan, heat 1 cup PJ Magic to boiling with a small cinnamon stick and 2 whole cloves. Strain into mug and discard cloves. Garnish with an orange or lemon wedge. Makes 1 drink.

PRUNE ALEX

A better Brandy Alexander takes a California twist. Guests will be intrigued. Prune juice is your secret.
1 8-ounce serving

1/4 cup chilled prune
   juice
3 tablespoons whip-
   ping cream
1&1/2 ounces brandy
   or vodka
1 teaspoon *each* sugar
   and cocoa powder
2 or 3 ice cubes

Combine all ingredients, except ice cubes, in electric blender, and blend thoroughly. Add ice cubes; blend until smooth and frothy. Pour into chilled stemmed glass.

PRUNE ORCHARD ENERGY NOG
About 3 cups

1 cup unflavored, low-
 fat yogurt
2/3 cup pitted prunes
2/3 cup apple juice
1 egg
1 tablespoon creamy
 peanut butter
1 tablespoon wheat
 germ (optional)
8 ice cubes

Blend all ingredients, except ice cubes, until smooth in electric blender. Scrape sides of container. With motor running, add ice cubes one at a time; blend until smooth.

THE TEA TODDY

Serve this fragrant pick-me-up warm or chilled, as the weather suggests.
2 8-ounce servings

1 cup prune juice
1 cup tea, brewed or
   instant
1 orange slice, halved
1 cinnamon stick,
   halved
4 whole cloves
Honey

In small saucepan, combine all ingredients except honey. Bring to boil. Reduce heat and simmer gently 3 minutes. To serve, strain into 2 cups, discarding cloves and dividing fruit equally. Stir in honey to taste.

MISCELLANEOUS

APPLE-SPICE GRIDDLE CAKES

Try these high-fiber pancakes for an autumn brunch or family dinner. The topping is great on waffles, too.
12 4-inch pancakes

1 cup flour
1/2 cup *each* whole-wheat flour and unprocessed bran (not cereal)
2 teaspoons *each* baking soda and sugar
1 teaspoon salt
2 cups buttermilk
2 eggs, lightly beaten
2 tablespoons (1/4 stick) butter, melted
1 cup pitted prunes, chopped

Apple-Spice Topping:
1 cup unsweetened apple sauce
1/3 cup pitted prunes, finely chopped
1/2 teaspoon cinnamon

In bowl, combine flours, bran, baking soda, sugar, and salt. Stir in buttermilk, eggs, butter, and prunes; mix with fork just to blend. Drop by large spoonfuls onto hot, nonstick skillet lightly oiled or sprayed with vegetable cooking spray. Cook over medium heat until golden brown on both sides, turning once. Serve hot with Apple-Spice Topping.

To make apple-spice topping: In small saucepan, combine apple sauce, prunes, and cinnamon. Heat to warm through.

Note: Cooked, cooled pancakes can be individually wrapped and frozen for a quick breakfast when you don't have time to cook. Simply unwrap and pop into your toaster to thaw and reheat.

BLUE-RIBBON PRUNE CHUTNEY

A county-fair classic, this chutney is delicious with hamburger, pork, or poultry. Served with cream cheese and crackers, it's an unusual hors d'oeuvre, too.
About 2 pints

2 cups diced, tart
  green apples
1&1/2 cups sliced
  onions
1 cup diced green bell
  pepper
1 garlic clove, crushed
3/4 cup white vinegar
3/4 cup sugar
2 cups pitted prunes,
  halved
1 teaspoon dry
  mustard
1/2 teaspoon *each* salt
  and ground ginger
1/4 teaspoon freshly
  ground pepper

In large saucepan, combine apples, onions, pepper, garlic, vinegar, and sugar. Bring to boil over medium heat. Reduce heat and simmer, stirring occasionally, about 15 minutes until vegetables are tender. Mix in remaining ingredients. Simmer about 10 minutes, stirring occasionally, until mixture is thick like jam.

Cool and refrigerate, covered. Or pour into canning jars and seal according to manufacturer's instructions. Process in hot-water bath for 15 minutes. Store in cool place.

BRANDIED PRUNES

Although brandied prunes are available in most gourmet shops, creative cooks will enjoy making their own. Serve brandied prunes as a dessert or as a topping on ice cream, custard, or rice pudding.

4 cups pitted prunes

1/4 cup superfine sugar

2 cinnamon sticks

1&1/2 cups brandy

1/2 cup strongly brewed tea

1 whole piece crystallized ginger

Place prunes in large glass bowl. Add sugar, cinnamon sticks, brandy, tea, and ginger. Mix well. Cover and let stand at room temperature 1 week before serving. Store, covered, in the refrigerator for up to 2 months. Remove spices before serving.

CRUNCHY PRUNE MIX

Both crunchy and chewy, this mix is perfect for the trail, picnics, or parties.
6 cups

1 cup *each* whole
natural almonds,
shredded coconut,
and sunflower
seeds, toasted
2 cups pitted prunes,
coarsely chopped
1 cup dried apples,
coarsely chopped

In large bowl, combine all ingredients; blend evenly. Store in airtight container for up to 2 weeks.

Note: To toast almonds, coconut, and sunflower seeds, place them in 3 separate pans. Toast in preheated 325° oven for 15 to 20 minutes; stir several times and remove when lightly browned.

East-West Barbecue Glaze

This piquant Asian glaze is spiked with red pepper. Try it as a table sauce for burgers, poultry, chops—sensational.
About 1&1/4 cups

1/4 cup finely chopped onion

1&1/2 teaspoons ground ginger

2 garlic cloves, minced

1 tablespoon oil

1/2 cup prune juice

1/4 cup distilled white vinegar

6 tablespoons sweet orange marmalade

1 teaspoon crushed red pepper

1/4 teaspoon salt (optional)

1 tablespoon cornstarch

2 tablespoons water

In saucepan over low heat, sauté onion, ginger, and garlic in oil for 5 minutes. Stir in prune juice, vinegar, marmalade, red pepper, and salt. Bring to boil, stirring; boil 1 minute. Dissolve cornstarch in water; stir into prune-juice mixture. Cook and stir until thickened, about 2 minutes. Store in covered container in refrigerator. Use as a basting sauce and glaze for barbecued or broiled meats and poultry.

FRUIT AND NUT SPREAD

About 2/3 cup

1 package (3 ounces)
cream cheese, soft-
ened
2 tablespoons orange
juice
1/2 teaspoon grated
orange peel
1/4 cup pitted prunes,
chopped
3 tablespoons walnuts,
chopped

In small bowl, beat cream cheese with juice and peel until smooth. Mix in prunes and nuts. Cover and chill to blend flavors. Use as a spread for whole-grain crackers or bread.

Fruit Cheese Log

An unusual addition to a cocktail party.
1 log

1 package (8 ounces)
  cream cheese, room
  temperature
3 cups grated jack
  cheese, room tem-
  perature
1/2 teaspoon salt
1 teaspoon caraway
  seeds
1/4 cup dry sherry
1/2 cup *each* pitted
  prunes and dried
  apricots, finely
  chopped
3/4 cup walnuts, finely
  chopped

Beat cream cheese until smooth. Combine with jack cheese, salt, caraway seeds, dry sherry, prunes, and apricots. Shape into a roll and cover with walnuts. Wrap roll in plastic wrap and chill in refrigerator until firm. Serve with crackers.

Note: The cheese log must be brought to room temperature before serving.

LUMBERJACK FLAPJACKS

Here is an old favorite of American lumber-jacks: flapjacks topped with molasses and spicy prune sauce.
2 cups sauce, a dozen 4-inch pancakes

Spicy Prune Sauce:

2 cups pitted prunes
1&3/4 cups water
1 teaspoon cinnamon
1/4 teaspoon ground
  ginger
Pinch salt
3 tablespoons molas-
  ses

Oatmeal Flapjacks:

1&1/2 cups buttermilk
3/4 cup rolled oats
1 egg
1/2 cup flour
1/2 teaspoon *each* salt
  and baking soda
1 tablespoon molasses
Butter or margarine

To make spicy prune sauce: In 2-quart saucepan, combine all sauce ingredients except molasses. Cook over medium heat, stirring occasionally, until prunes are tender, about 10 minutes. Stir in molasses; simmer 3 minutes.

To make oatmeal flapjacks: In large bowl, mix buttermilk and oats. Beat in remaining ingredients. Place lightly oiled griddle or skillet over medium heat. Ladle 3 tablespoons batter onto griddle for each flapjack. Cook until lightly browned, about 2 minutes on each side. Serve hot with warm prune sauce.

NORWEGIAN FRUIT SOUP

When friends join you on a summer evening, serve this chilled soup with a variety of cheeses and crackers.
4 servings

1/2 cup *each* pitted prunes, dried peaches, dried apples, and dried apricots, chopped
1/2 cup raisins
3 cups water
1/2 lemon, sliced
1 tablespoon quick-cooking tapioca
1/4 teaspoon salt
1/2 to 1/3 cup sugar
1 stick cinnamon

Mix all ingredients in saucepan and simmer until all fruits are tender, about 30 to 40 minutes. While cooking, watch the ratio of water to fruit; sometimes more liquid is needed during simmering. Add liquid to desired consistency. Remove lemon and cinnamon stick before serving.

OLD-FASHIONED PRUNE BUTTER

This easy fruit butter will dress up toast or hot muffins. It's wonderful as a cake or pastry filling, too.
About 2 pints

4 cups pitted prunes

2 cups orange juice

1/4 cup light-brown
  sugar

1/2 cup water

1 tablespoon grated
  orange peel

In large saucepan, combine prunes, juice, and sugar. Bring to boil over medium heat. Reduce heat and simmer 10 minutes, stirring occasionally. Cool slightly. Combine water and prune mixture in container of electric blender. Blend until smooth, scraping sides as needed.

Return prune puree to saucepan; mix in orange peel. Cook and stir over low heat 5 to 10 minutes until mixture is the consistency of thick jam. Store covered in refrigerator or spoon into canning jars and seal according to manufacturer's instructions. Process in hot-water bath for 15 minutes. Store in cool place.

PEACHY CHUTNEY

Very spicy! Great with chicken curry, lamb kebabs, or pita bread stuffed with curried rice salad. Spread on a block of cream cheese with crackers for a quick hors d'oeuvre.
4 cups

1 can (16 ounces)
  sliced peaches with
  juice
1/2 cup currants
1 can (8 ounces) un-
  peeled apricots with
  juice
1 cup pitted prunes
1 can (8 ounces) pear
  halves with juice
1/2 cup molasses
1/2 cup white *or* red
  wine vinegar
1/2 teaspoon salt
1 tablespoon curry
  powder
1 teaspoon ground
  ginger
1 teaspoon Dijon mus-
  tard
1/4 cup cornstarch
1/2 cup cold water

Combine all ingredients, except cornstarch and water, in large saucepan. Bring to a boil and simmer for 45 minutes, stirring occasionally.

In small bowl, combine cornstarch and water and stir to dissolve. Add to cooked chutney and cook over medium heat, stirring constantly until thickened. Pour chutney into clean jars and store in refrigerator.

PRUNE AND RAISIN SAUCE

This tangy sauce adds pizzazz to ham, chicken, pork, or duck.
Makes 2 cups

1 cup pitted prunes
1/2 cup raisins
2 tablespoons lemon
   juice
1 tablespoon finely
   grated lemon peel
8 whole cloves
1/4 teaspoon *each* cin-
   namon and allspice
1/2 teaspoon nutmeg
Dash of cardamom
1 cup water
1/2 cup sugar
1/2 cup red wine
   vinegar
1 cup raisins

Mix prunes, 1/2 cup of raisins, and lemon juice and peel with spices in medium-size saucepan. Add enough water to cover and cook over moderate heat until prunes have softened and water has reduced by half, about 15 minutes. Remove and discard cloves.

Place mixture in bowl of food processor. Puree until smooth. Return to saucepan and add sugar, vinegar, and 1 cup of raisins. Cook, stirring frequently, until sauce is heated through.

PRUNE-APPLE BUTTER

This high-fiber, fat-free spread is a healthy alternative to butter. Too delicious to keep to yourself, so make extra for friends.
About 3&1/2 cups

2&1/2 cups pitted prunes
3 medium, tart green apples, peeled, cored, and quartered
1&1/2 cups un-sweetened apple juice
1/3 cup crystallized ginger
1 teaspoon lemon juice

In 3-quart saucepan, combine fruits, apple juice, and ginger. Bring to boil; reduce heat, cover, and simmer gently 10 minutes. Uncover and continue to cook, stirring occasionally, until fruits are tender and liquid is almost completely absorbed, 10 to 15 minutes. Remove from heat; stir in lemon juice. Blend smooth, using food processor or electric blender. Cool. Store covered in refrigerator up to 3 weeks. Use as a spread for toast or muffins.

PRUNE BUTTER

2 cups

2&2/3 cups pitted
   prunes

Finely grated peel of 1
   orange

1 cup sugar

1/4 teaspoon *each*
   ground allspice,
   ginger, nutmeg, and
   cloves

1/2 teaspoon cinna-
   mon

1/8 teaspoon ground
   cardamom

Combine prunes, orange peel, sugar, and enough water to cover in medium-size saucepan. Bring to a boil; simmer for 15 minutes. In food processor or blender, puree prunes.

In same saucepan, combine prune puree with sugar and spices; cook over moderate heat until thick. After prune butter cools to room temperature, cover tightly and store in refrigerator for up to 2 months.

PRUNE FRITTERS

The French call them beignets. *The English call them fritters. But whatever the name, prunes dipped in a light batter and fried golden are heavenly.*
40 fritters (4 or 5 per serving)

2 cups pitted prunes

1/3 cup whole almonds, toasted

1/2 cup port *or* orange juice

3/4 cup flour

1/4 cup cornstarch

3/4 cup water

1 egg white, stiffly beaten

1/4 cup powdered sugar combined with 1/4 teaspoon cinnamon

Oil for deep frying

Sour cream (optional)

With knife point, make a small slit in prunes and insert an almond in each. Place in shallow bowl and toss with port or juice. Cover and set aside several hours, stirring occasionally.

In small, deep bowl, whisk together flour, cornstarch, and water; fold in egg white. In small bowl, combine sugar and cinnamon; set aside. In 2-quart saucepan, heat 3 inches oil to 375°. Drain prunes and dip into batter, drain excess, and deep-fry, a few at a time, until crisp and golden, about 3 minutes. Drain on paper towels. Serve fritters hot, dusted with cinnamon sugar. Serve with sour cream, if desired.

PRUNE VODKA

If your brunch menu traditionally includes Screwdrivers, try substituting this unusual vodka. It also would be a grand finale at your next dinner party.

1/2 cup pitted prunes, quartered

2 cups vodka

Combine prunes and vodka in a glass bowl. Cover with plastic wrap and place bowl in a dark, cool area for 6 weeks. Gently shake bowl occasionally to blend mixture. Strain and discard prunes before serving.

This recipe can easily be doubled.

SHELAGH'S COCK-A-LEEKIE SOUP

A good friend who was raised in Glasgow gave us this recipe for a traditional Scottish soup.
4 to 6 servings

1 large chicken with
  giblets
8 cups cold water
2 teaspoons salt
2 whole cloves
8 peppercorns
1 large onion,
  chopped
6 leeks, split, cleaned,
  and shredded
6 *each* pitted prunes
  and dried apricots,
  chopped
2 tablespoons un-
  cooked long-grain
  white rice
1 tablespoon chopped
  parsley
Freshly ground pepper

Put chicken and giblets in a large pot. Add water and seasonings and bring slowly to a boil. Simmer 45 minutes, occasionally skimming fat. Remove and discard cloves and peppercorns. Add onion, leeks, prunes, apricots, and rice and continue to simmer until chicken is tender. Remove chicken and giblets from broth. Shred from bones as much meat as wanted in soup and return to broth. Skim any fat from soup and add parsley. Add pepper and salt to taste. The remaining chicken is traditionally served as the entrée.

Note: You can stretch this recipe to serve a crowd by adding canned chicken broth, doubling the quantities of vegetables, fruits, and rice, and using all the chicken.

SPICY APRICOT-PRUNE GLAZE

The sweetness of prunes and the tanginess of apricots compliment each other in this zesty glaze.
2 cups

1/3 cup *each* dried apricots and pitted prunes
1/4 cup raisins
1&1/2 cups water
2/3 cup white wine vinegar
1/4 cup Dijon mustard
1/2 cup honey
2 tablespoons (1/4 stick) butter
1/4 cup minced shallots *or* red onion
1 teaspoon *each* salt and freshly ground pepper

In medium-size heavy saucepan, combine fruits with water. Bring to a boil and simmer for 15 minutes, uncovered, reducing the liquid by half. In food processor, puree the fruits with the remaining liquid. Add vinegar, mustard, and honey, combining well. In another medium-size saucepan, melt butter. Add shallots to pan and sauté until softened. Add the pureed mixture, salt, and pepper and bring to a boil. Simmer uncovered for 8 minutes or until thickened. To enhance flavor of pork, chicken, or ham, brush glaze on meat or poultry during last third of its roasting time.

This recipe, if covered and chilled, keeps for up to 2 weeks.

SWISS BREAKFAST MUESLI

Muesli *(pronounced muse-lee) is a nutritious combination of fruits, nuts, and oats developed around the turn of the century by Dr. Bircher-Benner in his health clinic in Switzerland.*
6 servings (about 4 cups)

1&1/2 cups rolled oats

1&1/2 cups water

2 cups shredded, unpeeled apple

1&1/2 cups pitted prunes, halved

2 tablespoons *each* honey and lemon juice

1/2 teaspoon cinnamon

Fresh fruits (sliced banana, apple, pineapple, orange segments)

Chopped walnuts

Combine oats, water, shredded apple, prunes, honey, lemon juice, and cinnamon. Cover and refrigerate overnight. In the morning, spoon some of the muesli into a cereal bowl. Top with your choice of fresh fruit and walnuts. Serve with milk or a dollop of unflavored yogurt, if desired. You can store muesli in a covered container in refrigerator for several days.

ACKNOWLEDGMENTS

We thank the California Prune Board for the support and encouragement it gave us while we wrote *The Prune Gourmet*. It provided us with the following recipes:

Germantown Beef Stew

Prune Orchard Beef Stew

Country Baked Spareribs

Chicken Breasts with Curried Vegetables

California Harvest Stuffing

Harvest Stuffing

Bon Bon Fruit Compote

Prune Citrus Bowl

Rubyfruit Prune Compote

High-Fiber Prune Muffins

Rise 'n' Shine Breakfast Muffins

Hearty Prune Bread

Prune-Crumb Coffee Cake

California Batter Bread

Autumn Prune-Apple Cake

Apple-Prune Dowdy

Spirited Prune Bread Pudding

Chewy Chocolate Nuggets

Early Riser Prune Cookies

Plump Prune Pillows

Good Morning Bracer

PJ Magic

Prune Alex

Prune Orchard Energy Nog

The Tea Toddy

Apple-Spice Griddle Cakes

Blue-Ribbon Prune Chutney

Crunchy Prune Mix

East-West Barbecue Glaze

Fruit and Nut Spread

Lumberjack Flapjacks

Old-Fashioned Prune Butter

Prune-Apple Butter

Prune Fritters

Swiss Breakfast Muesli

Prune and Walnut Layer Cake. From *Maida Heatter's Book of Great American Desserts* by Maida Heatter. Text copyright © 1983, 1984, 1985 by Maida Heatter. Reprinted by permission of Alfred A. Knopf.

INDEX